Play Therapy in the Outdoors

Play Therapy in the Outdoors

Taking Play Therapy out of the Playroom and into Natural Environments

Alison Chown

Foreword by Sara Knight

Jessica Kingsley *Publishers*
London and Philadelphia

Disclaimer
Before practising play therapy outdoors, readers should always seek legal advice to ensure compliance with the health and safety regulations that govern outdoor activities with children. Neither the authors nor the publisher take any responsibility for any consequences of any action taken as a result of the information contained in this book.

First published in 2014
by Jessica Kingsley Publishers
73 Collier Street
London N1 9BE, UK
and
400 Market Street, Suite 400
Philadelphia, PA 19106, USA

www.jkp.com

Copyright © Alison Chown 2014
Foreword copyright © Sara Knight 2014

Library of Congress Cataloging in Publication Data
A CIP catalog record for this book is available from the Library of Congress

British Library Cataloguing in Publication Data
A CIP catalogue record for this book is available from the British Library

ISBN 978 1 84905 408 9
eISBN 978 0 85700 805 3

Printed and bound in Great Britain

For Marjorie and Eric who gave us freedom in childhood and a passion for being outdoors and for Rhiannon and Jack to whom I appear to have passed this on.
May they too hand it on to their own in years to come.

Rhiannon and Jack

For I have walked in the sunshine, danced in the rain
I have run with the wind, I need to do these things again and again
I need to look to my horizons and see my spirit fly
I believe I should breathe in the open sky, high, high, high,
I believe I should breathe in the open sky

Words by Sue Beckers, 2005
From the song arranged and performed by Slipstream,
Sophy Burleigh, Penny Dunscombe, Bryony Penman and Sue Beckers

Contents

Figures

Foreword

From very similar early experiences roaming across the fields with a group of other children, through teacher training and work in schools, my life's journey has parallels with Ali's. But I encountered Forest School first, and have come to green therapies later. I, too, had a seminal moment observing a four-year-old child engaged in deep play outside, with a stick rather than a stone, a moment that reinforced an intuitive conviction that being outside is the best place to learn – to learn about self, others and the world, and to learn to find a balance in our lives. Since then I have been privileged to participate in Forest School experiences with children and adults of all ages, and seen its transformational power. Young children find ways to be, establishing healthy habits that will stand by them for life. Not for nothing did the Jesuits say, 'Give me a child until he is seven and I will give you the man.' What we now know about brain development tells us that habits and behaviours established early in our lives are hard to change. Young trainee teachers and nursery nurses discover that learning is such fun outside, that mud is a good thing and getting wet is not dangerous in itself. Older adults relax (regress?) and reconnect with the deeper interconnectedness of Gaia (the personification of Earth; the great Mother of all from Greek mythology). When asked to summarise a week outside with an artefact made with the resources around them, they create keys, windows, dreamcatchers and webs – all symbols of seeing and feeling in deeper and more meaningful ways.

In my darkest moments following the sudden death of my dear husband I have drawn on the earth for strength, walking the fields and hills to seek a new equilibrium. The healing balm of nature is important to all ages. But for our children, those whose life experiences have been so short that the percentage of the experience that has not been beneficial or has been damaging can be huge, Mother Nature can work with us to sooth and heal. More than that, we can work in and with nature to help children to develop new and better ways of moving forward in the world. Visualise two children leading another who is blindfold through a wood. The leaders are blind, but from their own experiences among the trees, they have established an 'internal map' and are sharing their knowledge of the wood with a classmate (Knight 2011, p.128). What a positive way to develop your sense of who you are in your world! It is my hope that this book will inspire readers to go forward to work with nature in the best ways for them and for the benefit of the people they encounter.

Sara Knight
Deputy Chairman of the UK Forest School Association
and author of books about Forest School

Author's Notes

A Word About Theory

That theory and research are important elements of our practice, I am of no doubt. That theory should serve to clarify and illuminate our practice rather than hamper us with inflexibility, I am equally clear.

I have always regarded myself as a practitioner, my own definition of this being twofold: first, I have always been 'hands on', working directly with children, young people, their families and the people who support them. Second, I learn constantly from that practice, from all those with whom I work. Underpinning this is a wealth of theory and research which has given me knowledge and understanding in order to make sense of that which comes from practice and which I instinctively know works but often have little idea why!

My own work across the years has been significantly influenced by a number of 'theoretical perspectives'; the attachment work of John Bowlby, Mary Ainsworth, Dan Hughes and Heather Geddes; Carl Rogers's ideas of democratic education expressed in his book *Freedom to Learn*; Virginia Axline and Gary Landreth's approaches to play therapy; Sue Jennings's EPR paradigm; the principles of the Forest School ethos; and the developmental approach of THRIVE, all of which are referenced elsewhere in this book. Alongside these sit another diverse range of ideas and thinking encompassing both education and therapeutic practice which have had an influence on me and which are discussed within this book.

Over the years, my own reading of both educational and therapeutic texts, many of them regarded as 'seminal', has often left me feeling that I have undergone an academic exercise to test my ability to comprehend weighty material, and more often than not I get a sense of having failed – failed, because much of what I have read has not stuck with me. I have always joked about being a 'concrete' learner and what I think I mean by this is that theory only makes sense to me when I can apply it directly to the practice I am engaged in so that I can gain meaning from it.

Trevithick (2005), discussing knowledge in relation to social work practice, outlines three 'interconnected' areas: theoretical knowledge (or theory), factual knowledge and practice knowledge (knowledge in practice), and notes that although all are important, the first, theoretical knowledge, 'carries considerable weight because of the importance of the link between theory and practice' (p.25). The perspectives discussed above are the foundations of my practice and thinking and are, I believe, what makes this book accessible to and appropriate for a wide range of practitioners.

So there is knowledge which comes actively to us through our everyday practice interactions and is two way so that we both share our knowledge with and share knowledge from clients, colleagues and others. There is knowledge that comes to us from theory and from our reading and discussions, from lectures, training from others and from workshops and conferences. Finally, there is knowledge that comes from our own life experiences and our very act of living. Cattananch (2003) notes that our individual experiences and our learning from both these and theory will influence and shape our particular approach and discusses Meldrum's suggestion (1996) that it is practice which gives rise to exploration of theory and that rather than theory being imposed on practice, it should underpin what we have come to know through our experience with clients.

The integration of these forms of dynamic knowledge is immensely powerful to our understanding of, or knowing about ourselves, those within our personal lives, our clients, their families and our colleagues. We need to have confidence in this knowledge and use it to inform our work, to facilitate collaboration rather than competition. Porter, writing on the theory and practice of behaviour in schools (2006), notes, 'We all develop ideas – that is theories – however this process of personal theory building is more efficient and comprehensive when informed in advance by theoretical knowledge' (p.5). However, in recognising the place of theory in our practice, we must not lose confidence in our own abilities to generate theories or our practice will become static and bland rather than dynamic and creative. A friend once said to me that doing something just because we have always done it that way is no reason at all for doing it. We need to recognise that theory is not the sole realm of academics but can be born out of our 'wonderings' about everyday practice with our clients, and so as practitioners we can become theorists and give voice to these wonderings with confidence.

Acknowledgements

My thanks go to all those children, young people and their families who have given up their stories over the years and to my many colleagues who have shared their knowledge, wisdom and experience. Thank you to Jan and Abadha for Burning Bird and everything after, and to Charlotte and Pam for their friendship, encouragement and belief.

During the writing of this book, Sarah, Janette and my daughter Rhiannon have given their time to read and comment; I am grateful for their honesty and enthusiasm and my thanks also go to my son Jack for his design and technical support and to Lisa Clarke at JKP for her tolerance of many questions and her guidance through the process.

Special gratitude and thanks go to Penny for her friendship, support, encouragement and wisdom, to Sara Knight for understanding the concept and to Dr Sue Jennings for the inspiration she is.

And finally, thank you, John, for your encouragement, support, patience and love, for all the 'lively' discussions we have had and for sharing Folly Farm with me.

Introduction

...best of all has to be jumping in puddles and splashing oneself and playing in real mud after it has been raining. It is important to have contact with nature and for damaged children, it can be a very healing experience.

(Jennings 2011, p.163)

When I was little, I seem to remember spending so much time out of doors; in the garden, across the fields, at the 'rec' and down at the allotment with my big brother. I remember our house and what it was like inside, but most of all I remember being outside.

The author as a young child

We lived in a council house with a big, long garden. We had a shed and a coal house, a lean-to greenhouse at the back, a flowering cherry, a greengage tree and a vegetable garden which ran down either side of the path to the school playing fields behind. It was here that I first discovered the absolute joy, which I still experience now as an adult, of seeing how a tiny dry seed could magically turn into a green shoot and then grow into something we could eat. At the back of the house I remember big pink peonies whose petals I steeped in water to make perfume, and I remember oversized orange poppies, tall purple irises, yellow daffodils in the spring, warm sunshine, bitter winter winds and frost inside the windows. It was elemental, free ranging and full of stark contrasts – a real feast for the senses.

Then, we rode our bikes without helmets, roamed free over the fields for hours on end and played out in the dark. It wasn't idyllic. I burned my hand in a pile of smouldering ashes left in a field and cut my leg so badly on barbed wire that it required a visit to casualty and left me with tramline scars on the back of my calf. We got chased by a farmer with a shotgun and a big dog, fell off our bikes and regularly grazed our knees and skinned our elbows. But we also breathed fresh air, exercised our bodies and worked out how to solve problems, take risks and get on with each other.

I know it is easy to see our own childhood through those well-known 'rose-tinted spectacles' but I am not one who hankers for the past. I have embraced technological change and own two mobile phones, a laptop, a notebook and a diesel car. I like nothing better than an evening in with the iPlayer! I do, however, think that we have a tendency to box our children in now. We talk to them about saving the planet and the destruction of the rain forests but shield them from the perceived danger of our own beautiful landscapes. In 2012, the National Trust published a list of '50 things to do before you are 11¾', which included such things as build a den, climb a tree, run around in the rain, play conkers and dam a stream, all things which children might naturally do without direction if left to their own devices in outdoor spaces.

During the summer I watched a small boy of about three at the edge of a very shallow river which ran into the sea. He picked up a big stone and tottered to the water's edge to try and toss it into the water. The stone was heavy and it merely dropped down about 30cm away. He retrieved it and tried again, but this time he gave a little hop as he tossed the stone. It landed farther away, but still short of the water so he persevered, increasing the height of his hop until it was almost a jump and after several more attempts, the stone splashed into the water. He chuckled loudly, smiling from ear to ear and hopped about excitedly, flapping his arms in pure joy. I laughed out loud too; it was impossible not to in the face of such unadulterated pleasure. In these days of mindfulness, this was true living in the moment! Then he looked around for another stone, chose one which was slightly smaller than the last and began all over again. His parents were close enough to keep him safe, but had they been right beside him, it is likely that his exploration and problem solving would have become adult directed and the outcome would have been nowhere near as joyful.

Undoubtedly our towns now have far less green space and fewer areas that are traffic free but when I recently saw a training course advertised on 'Developing Risky Play' it made me realise how much we have softened our children's world, taken away the sharp edges and tried to keep them safe indoors. What we may inadvertently be teaching them, however, is to be scared of reality.

The virtual worlds of computer games and social networking media are very constructed and devoid of authentic emotional content. To gain 'friends', you do not have to have a face-to-face conversation about what you have in common that would inspire a friendship or discuss what transgressions have been committed for you to not want it to continue. You do not have to engage in any real social conversation, problem solving or conflict resolution, you can simply create or delete a 'friend' at the touch of a button, without even knowing them first.

Is it any wonder then that demands of actual relationships in the real world may be difficult for many people, old and young alike?

Real world thrills, excitement and risk are replaced by their electronic equivalents. However, there are very real differences; the electronic world is two-dimensional, provides limited sensory feedback, and is usually solitary and sedentary. It can offer an exciting escape from real life, but is no substitute for it…the time spent watching screens

> can take away from time spent actively engaging with people and things and excessive watching can impact on children's learning, health and well-being. (Tovey 2007, p.6)

As an adult, I have spent years working indoors in classrooms and offices, driving to meeting after meeting in my car or working at home and feeling restless and unsettled, despite enjoying most of my work. I have finally realised it is because I need to be outside, connecting with the natural world. This is not an attempt to shy away from work, but a deep-seated *need*. It has taken me until now really to appreciate how much this is part of who I am – never happier than when I am 'grubbing' in the earth planting seeds, walking the hills or the coastal path, or sitting on the beach watching the sun glistening on the water with a gentle breeze on my face. It is the sensory food of life and needs to be a varied diet of sights, sounds, smells, tastes and sensations on my body.

All humans need this; it is at our core and is deeply therapeutic to both our bodies and our minds. It feeds our spirit, soothes our soul and connects us to the earth's vital energy. It is our very own therapist in waiting. Yet somehow, there is now a disconnection between us and the land around us, that very earth on which we walk. Graham Bell, writing in his introduction to *The Permaculture Garden* (2004) suggests this is the result of the agricultural, industrial and technological revolutions that our society has undergone in recent times and notes that prior to this, most people passed the majority of their time with a direct connection to and a keen interest in their natural environment. This disconnection is resonant of the fractured relationships experienced by many of the children who come to play therapy, children who have no real sense of who they are physically, emotionally, cognitively and spiritually. We might say of them that they are not grounded in any way and although we may share a common understanding of the word, we may miss the relevance of it in relation to the changes Bell notes.

Within society, we are beginning to recognise this disconnection and to see again the part that the outdoors can play not only in our leisure activities but also in maintaining our mental and physical health, in bringing greater creativity to our children's education and in providing food to sustain our communities. In *Ecotherapy – the green agenda for mental health* (2007), MIND found that 90 per cent of those who took part in their green exercise activities noted that the combination of nature and exercise was most important in determining how they felt. The Forest School movement, originally brought to the UK from Denmark by staff from Bridgwater College in Somerset (Knight 2009), is now widespread, involving all ages and including family groups and those young people with social, emotional and behavioural needs and complex learning difficulties. In many areas of the country there is an increasing demand for allotments and an increase in the establishment of community gardens and orchards.

I trained as a teacher in the late 1970s and after four years working as a class teacher in a large primary school, I spent a year at Ingleborough Hall Outdoor Education Centre in the Yorkshire Dales National Park. It was a transformational year for me in a number of ways. First, it was the only time I had worked with children for whom English was not their first language; second, the experience provided for the children was residential and necessitated a different type of relationship to those I had so far developed with my classes and third, I realised what a powerful tool for learning and development the outdoor environment was. It also proved to be a great leveller in that, often, those with more outgoing and assertive personalities showed considerably more fear in a dark wet cave than one might have imagined they would and they discovered why co-operation was essential. Most of the children found that when your hands are almost numb from the cold, despite gloves and waterproofs, you need others to help you open your rucksack, take the top off your sandwich box or even undo the zip on your coat and trousers when you need to pee!

When I returned to classroom teaching, I found that my whole philosophy was different. I spent much more time developing real relationships with the children – relationships that were about them and who they were and not about how a teacher ought to relate to children. For the first time, I really began to think about how they learned and what would motivate them. I read Carl Rogers's (1983) book *Freedom to Learn for the 80's* and considered how to make my classroom and my teaching more democratic. I looked for opportunities to use the outdoor environment but found these more limited by school politics and procedures than I had anticipated, and the further I got from my own direct experience of working outdoors, the less clear my thinking remained about a 'rationale' for doing so. What I now realise is that had I had the time and the motivation earlier in my career to research more widely, I might have discovered the work of Froebel, Steiner, Montessori and Pestalozzi, the 'progressive' educators. However, it was many years before my desire to underpin with relevant theory what I was beginning instinctively to 'know' worked in practice led me to these and later, and most importantly for me, the Forest School movement.

At that time in the late 1970s, although teacher training looked at what was broadly called 'child development', the understanding about attachment, relationships and how our social and emotional well-being underpins our availability for learning was nowhere near as developed and prevalent in wider educational thinking as it is today. During the last 15 years of my teaching career, it has been this which has guided my practice as a specialist teacher for children with social, emotional and behavioural needs. Working with some of our most 'challenging' children within both the mainstream and specialist sectors of the education system, the notion that before you can develop good social skills, empathy, motivation and self-regulation you need a good level of self-awareness has become paramount. However, for the most part, schools have struggled to make this kind of provision, due partly to a lack of understanding of a more holistic educational approach and partly because the exacting toll children with social, emotional and behavioural (SEB) needs take on teachers and support staff tends to leave them bereft of energy and creativity.

In supporting staff as an advisory teacher for SEB I felt more often than not that I could only really offer more of the same school-based interventions which had already failed to meet the children's needs and were in fact often compounding their difficulties. Supporting agencies that might be able to offer therapeutic work such as the Child and Adolescent Mental Health Services (CAMHS), often had long waiting lists and a process that appeared to make the ability of the parent to attend appointments the focus of support for the child. It was my frustration with the lack of a more therapeutic input available for these children within their school setting that led me towards more therapeutic interventions.

As a play therapist, I was trained to work only within the playroom to ensure confidentiality for the client and to maintain ethical practice. In fact, for those who trained me, my thoughts about moving out of the playroom into the great outdoors would probably appear to be an anathema to the very idea of safe therapeutic practice. However, I think this is where we need to question who it is who has the need for this notion of only one containable space – our clients, or the therapists themselves? Does the strong and, to my mind, quite singular focus on confidentiality obscure the issues of therapist power and control? For me, it is the very relationship between the therapist and the client that is the safe 'container' for the work and as such, the environment in which the therapy takes place can be different and can be outside a walled and potentially clinical playroom.

This idea to move my play therapy practice outside had been forming in my mind for some time and the ethos of the Forest School movement has been a strong influence. I have talked to my peers who are therapists, some of whom have highlighted the possible conflict with the idea of the safe therapeutic space but most of whom have been enthused by my thinking, as has my supervisor. Some of you who are reading this may disagree with what I propose, but for many others there will be a resonance, an understanding that to shackle children to the playroom is to deny them their world.

In my therapeutic work I would never want to compromise or endanger either my client or myself but now, having worked with many 'complex' children and young people, I believe the idea of the playroom being the only safe space to offer containment needs to be challenged, particularly if we are to hold the child and their needs as central to the process. Much of my work has been with children and young people with profound and multiple learning difficulties (PMLD) who have significant developmental delay and are in need of early sensory experiences. While my playroom offers a range of resources designed to stimulate the senses and provide those relevant experiences, I can only create a limited and somewhat 'sterile' experience of textures, smells, sights, tastes and sensations (Santostefano 2004) and although the space might be containing, the big, gross motor movement so important to early development is restricted.

When a child's responses to the playroom have resulted in them not wanting to enter it, and we have remained outside, the natural elements of sun, wind, rain, warmth and cold have, I believe, offered a much more real sensory experience. If we use play in therapy because it is a child's natural mode of communication, then why do we not consider it appropriate to use the outdoor environment which is a much more natural playroom for the child than a confined indoor space?

One of the tenets of non-directive play therapy is supporting a healthy developmental trajectory as defined by Jennings (1999, 2011) through her embodiment, projection and role paradigm (EPR) and her theory of neuro-dramatic play (NDP). She suggests that the development of the body self teaches us about how we connect physically with the world around us and how we learn about our total physicality. Orbach (2003, p.27) when discussing how we develop our body self notes that, 'The body that is not received, the body that has no body to meet in its development becomes a body that is as precarious, fractured, defended, and unstable as a precarious psyche'. Our understanding of our body's capabilities, our relationship with it, our feelings about it and our direct experience of living within it require us to have experienced the body of an attuned other who held us, soothed us, rocked us, touched our skin with their skin and whose hands and body gave us a template for gentle, intimate and appropriate touch.

Our first year of life is full of sensory play and inter-play and it is this sensory experience which validates our relationship with the environment so that we can make choices about what we like and dislike, what soothes or stimulates us. We make sense of our world and discover its rules and social meaning. Our early relationships need to be playful, rhythmic and dramatic and touch all of our senses. The meaning a child makes while negotiating early developmental needs is constructed and expressed through non-verbal ways, including tactile and kinaesthetic perceptions and actions (Santostefano 2004), which leave the child with memories which are embedded within their sensory system and which therefore need sensory experiences in order to be processed and re-worked. It is this experience of a concrete, physical and visceral relationship with the 'real' world, through sensory feedback and experiential learning, which provides us with the 'map' for building relationships with people.

If therapy takes place in an external environment, the relationship between the therapist and the child provides the containment necessary to hold the therapeutic framework. It is the very space between them that bonds them together in a much more equal relationship with the outdoor space that neither 'owns' but to which both can have access. It is this relationship with the environment which becomes the primary attachment relationship, and the environment takes on aspects of both the role of the therapist and the primary carer. This is the crucial factor, for if this happens, and the child learns that certain environments and activities can soothe and calm in the way the 'mother' can, then they have immediate, free and lifelong access to their own individual therapy; they know the 'nature mother'. This is not to say that in later life, overwhelming anxiety, fear, panic and distress will not need support from mental health services or the mediation of a therapist, but if, as human beings, we can regularly and easily access that which supports our good mental and emotional well-being, we are likely reduce the necessity for more acute intervention. We may also begin to develop a greater understanding of the interconnectedness we have with nature. As one adult who participated in the MIND ecotherapy project noted in relation to the outdoors:

> It improves my depression, helps me to be more motivated and gives me satisfaction in doing things. Since starting the project I have been able to improve on the quality of my life. Coming here has helped me overcome most of my problems. (2007)

However, in respect of this new relational paradigm for play therapy I have asked myself, 'Why stick your head above the parapet?' Bond (2004) suggests that there is a strong expectation that in order to extend practice and challenge or transform existing knowledge, practitioners in counselling and psychotherapy need to undertake research. As such, our own practice can be viewed as research and indeed the case study is a key practitioner research method which contributes to dynamic practice that is both reflective and reflexive.

There has often been resistance to research in the arts therapies (Grainger 1999), not least because of the issue of 'client confidentiality'. However, challenges to existing traditions of thinking are surely essential if our practice is to reflect the various and shifting needs of our client groups and also the prevailing culture within wider society. We are at a time when many key organisations and agencies are recognising that we need to get children outside again, that we have wrapped them in the cotton wool of perceived danger, calculated thorough risk assessment, rather than '...doing risk benefit assessments: to recognise the upside of risk' (Gill 2012) and the positive contribution that challenge can make to all aspects of our development throughout our lives.

This book will explore why and how we might move play therapy outside into the natural environment in a safe and ethical way which both protects our clients but also offers them what I believe to be a more powerful and holistic therapeutic experience, particularly relevant to the embodiment (E) stage of Jennings's EPR paradigm but applicable to most client groups.

For me as both a specialist teacher for children with social, emotional and behavioural difficulties (SEBD) and a play therapist whose client group includes young people with profound and multiple learning difficulties, it has been the synthesis of two modes of working; teaching and therapy and the philosophy of the Forest School movement and the Reggio Emilia approach that has inspired me think more dynamically and creatively about my therapeutic practice – to think 'outside the box' of one room and look towards the world beyond, which is after all the one we must all eventually learn to engage with.

This book will explore traditions of thinking about the outdoors and its use in both education and therapy. It will consider the principles and practice of Forest School, the nature of child development and the process of play therapy and how these can, together, inform a more holistic and real therapeutic pathway for children and young people to provide a 'bridge' that unites the co-constructed therapeutic alliance, the essence of the play therapy session, with the outdoors. It will consider how we might define ethical practice and challenge the widely held belief that the only safe space for play therapy is the playroom or clinic setting. As my own thinking comes from many years of working with children in educational settings, I will draw on research and theory that may be different to that more traditionally used in therapeutic circles.

If, through the reading of these pages, I only challenge your own thinking and in doing so, strengthen the principles of your current practice, then this book will have served its purpose. However, if after reading it, you are encouraged to open the doors of your playroom, take a walk outside and begin to consider the potential of the outdoor environment, then I and those who are within these pages will walk beside you and encourage you on your pathway of discovery.

Ali Chown, April 2013
From many beautiful open spaces

PART I

The Context and the Theory

Chapter 1

Traditions of Thinking
About the Outdoors

This chapter will explore some traditions of using the outdoor environment to promote good physical, emotional, spiritual and mental well-being. It will consider some of the many organisations which work with young people and the common philosophical strands that exist between these, progressive educationalists and those therapeutic approaches which use natural spaces. It will discuss principles common to the Forest School movement, the Reggio Emilia approach and play therapy and how the synthesis of these with educational theory and practice has informed my work in the outdoors.

In considering traditions of using the outdoors it is not my intention to provide a full and detailed historical account of our exploration of the benefits of being outside, but rather to explore some of the common themes in thinking over the last 250 years about how the outdoor environment might have a significant role to play in the emotional, social, mental and physical health and well-being of all. It is by no means an exhaustive list but these are the themes I personally have become aware of over the years and which have influenced my own thinking. It is an eclectic assortment!

Octavia Hill and the first social housing

The period of the Industrial Revolution, generally recognised as being between 1750 and 1830, saw a move away from an agrarian activity with its associated deep connection to the land towards an industrial, machine-driven economy, which in turn led to huge numbers of workers migrating from rural areas to towns and cities to take up work in factories and mills. This great influx of workers into urban areas resulted in overcrowded housing, characterised by poor sanitation and cramped conditions where disease was rife and access to green space and even fresh air almost non-existent. Those who were poorly paid, both in the newly established factories of the towns and cities and much of the remaining rural economy, lived in social conditions which Robert Owen, mill owner, social reformer and one of the architects of the co-operative movement, considered to be responsible for their 'corruption'. It was this recognition of the detrimental effect of the environment on body, mind, soul and spirit that led to what has become known as the Age of Reform. It was a period when both individual philanthropists and what we would now call pressure groups campaigned for reform of economic, constitutional, political and social issues, the latter of which were needed to deal with social problems and abuses arising from the huge growth of urban population (Briggs 2011).

One of the leading social reformers was Octavia Hill (1838–1912), who was also co-founder of the National Trust. Hill came from a family tradition of awareness of the deep divide between the monied and working classes. Her father James Hill, a banker, lost his bank during 1825 as a result of a national banking crisis, an experience which appeared to radicalise him and to give his daughter a 'sense of the occasional precariousness of middle class life (Hunt 2012). Following the death of his second wife, James Hill married Caroline Southwood Smith and it was her father's views on the injustices and inequalities within society that were influential in situating the Hills and their children firmly within the movement for social reform.

From an early age, Octavia was aware of the vast divide between rich and poor, and during her life she promoted the idea that good housing, recreation, open spaces and education were vital for individual and family happiness. In the 1870s, she met John Ruskin through a mutual friend, Hardwicke Rawnsley. Ruskin had been left an inheritance and Hill suggested that he use the money to establish the first social housing in an area of London called Paradise Place, also known as 'Little Hell'. Ruskin left the management of the three houses to Hill, and her approach of improving 'the people and the buildings together' in order that sections of society were not marginalised was the first step towards social inclusion (Clayton 2012).

Hill's management of the housing blocks was based on clear expectations of her tenants, supported by the building of empowering relationships with them and the setting aside of monies for repairs, the balance of which was given back to the tenants to decide how it should be spent. It is important to note that Hill's intention was not to 'do unto' the poor, but, as she herself suggests in an essay from Homes of the London Poor (1875, reprinted in 2010), 'to rouse habits of industry and effort without which they might finally sink – with which they might render themselves independent of me'. It is this sense of promoting autonomy that is common to therapeutic work with all ages today.

Along with her sister, Hill also went on to found the Kyrle Society with the aim of bringing beauty to the people as London developed and grew. The destruction of the surrounding open land and green spaces within the city contrasted starkly with Hill's belief that every house should have a garden, that children should attend education and have space to play in and that everyone needed access to the open air for a healthy life. In another of her essays, she writes that the creation of 'places to sit in, places to play in, places to stroll in and places to spend a day' are all necessary for 'a common inheritance from generation to generation…of a park or the common which a man shares with his neighbours without pauperising' (1875, p.29). Despite her early failure to save Swiss Cottage as green space for all and her subsequent period of illness and recovery, Hill returned to campaigning for 'pure earth, clean air and blue sky' (Clayton 2012, p.17), which led to the idea of 'green belt' land and the creation of large open spaces such as Vauxhall Park and Parliament Hill Fields. In 1895, in order to protect these outdoor spaces, Hill, Rawnsley and Robert Hunter together founded the National Trust for Places of Historic Interest or Natural Beauty, enabled by an Act of Parliament to hold lands in perpetuity so that everyone might access them for ever. It is known today as the National Trust.

The Garden City movement

The migration of workers from rural areas to towns and cities continued and three years after the birth of the National Trust, social reformer Ebenezer Howard published *Tomorrow A Peaceful Path to Real Reform*, republished in 1902 as *Garden Cities of Tomorrow*. Here again was the idea of access for all to green space and fresh air, not by reforming existing housing, but by the creation of 'new towns' – well-planned urban areas with green spaces surrounded by agricultural land to bring together the rural and the urban environments and provide an antidote to the living conditions which existed for the poor in cities, towns and countryside. This Garden City movement promoted good, affordable housing with gardens, away from the industrial area, with tracts of green space for all and saw the creation of a clean working environment as an essential aspect of healthy living.

The idea was for an area of housing and industry of around 1,000 acres (the urban) surrounded by agricultural land of around 5,000 acres (the rural), all of which would support a socially mixed population of 32,000. The architects for the first Garden City, built at Letchworth, Hertfordshire, and opened in 1903, were Barry Parker and Raymond Unwin whose designs became the blueprint for many other new towns worldwide. As with Hill's housing management, profits from the management and development of the land were put back into benefits for the community. This emphasis on the community and opportunities to contribute to its development was crucial to the sense of ownership by the people, a theme that was strongly echoed by the later movement for access to the countryside for leisure activities, particularly rambling, by those whose lives had been spent working in noisy, poorly lit and dangerous factories.

Access to the moorland and mountains – a working-class struggle

To see the context for this movement we need to go back to the time before the Industrial Revolution and consider the impact of a long series of enclosure acts. In his article 'A short history of enclosure in Britain', Fairlie notes that:

Over the course of a few hundred years, much of Britain's
land has been privatized – that is to say taken out of some
form of collective ownership and management and handed
over to individuals. Currently...nearly half the country is
owned by 0.06 per cent of the population ... [While] there
are many factors that have led to such extreme levels of land
concentration...the most blatant and the most contentious
has been enclosure. (2009, p.16)

Although the open field system and communal pastures of the
Middle Ages had been under attack for a long time, the pace of
land enclosure increased dramatically by the mid-18th century.
Initially this was to support the farming of sheep by the wealthier
land owners and much arable land was lost to pasture. However,
by the end of the 18th century, there was growing need to return
to food production to sustain the increasing population and there
was less need for pasture as imported cotton from the United States
and India was replacing wool in the mills and factories. Alongside
this, with the uniting of Scotland with England came the Highland
Clearances when, as Fairlie further notes, 'thousands of highlanders
were evicted from their holdings and shipped off to Canada or
carted off to Glasgow to make way for Cheviot sheep' (p.24). On
the moors of the Peak District and the Yorkshire Dales, much of the
land that had formerly been used for sheep was then used 'for the
business of grouse shooting, the sport of a tiny section of wealthy
people' (Rothman 2012, p.11).

The need of those from the overcrowded cities and towns to
access open spaces and fresh air became even more imperative in
the face of increasing unemployment and was characterised by the
growing numbers of working class ramblers and cyclists who made
their way out into the countryside at weekends. With the cost of
motor cars well out of their reach, they were served well by the
railways, which offered cheap tickets and excursions, and so the
'town dwellers lived for the weekend when they could go camping
in the country' (Rothman 2012, p.12). Alongside this, there was a
growing interest in rough camping and in 1893 the Co-operative
Holidays Association was formed with the purpose of arranging
rambling holidays. The huge popularity of rambling was shown
in the formation of a number of footpath associations or societies,

and in 1900 the first working-class rambling club, the Sheffield Clarion Ramblers, was formed. This was followed in 1905 by the formation in London of the Federation of Rambling Clubs. However, in the North of England, where the greatest industrial development had been centred, access to much of the moorland remained restricted and the surrounding publicly accessible areas soon became overcrowded, with the footpaths turning to muddy quagmires during wet weather. Despite the network of public paths around Kinder Scout in the Peak District, there was a huge area of moorland over which no public access was allowed, and in 1932, this was to be the scene of the most memorable of land trespasses, the Kinder Trespass, led by Benny Rothman.

Although the Commons Preservation Society was founded in 1865, it was not until 1884 that the liberal MP James Bryce had introduced the first 'Access to Mountains' Bill which would give the public the right to walk on uncultivated moorland. However, efforts to get the Bill passed through Parliament were severely frustrated by a ruthless lobby from the powerful landowners who wanted to restrict access to the public, in no small part to protect their grouse shooting activities, despite these only taking place on a small number of days each year. There had been several smaller but still quite sizable demonstrations against access restrictions from 1847 to 1930, but to no avail.

The British Workers' Sports Federation (BWSF), started in 1928 as a working-class organisation promoting sport for workers, had been mainly active in the London area on the issue of Sunday football, but in 1932 it began to organise open-air events in the North of England to introduce more young people to the countryside. From one of these meetings came the idea for the Mass Trespass (Rothman 2012). Although there was strong opposition from the Manchester Ramblers Federation, considered by the trespassers as a middle class organisation, the BWSF organisers were in no way deterred and on 24 April 1932 a group of some 400 ramblers set off from Hayfield and despite a confrontation with gamekeepers on the way as they moved onto the moorland, they gathered for a meeting at Ashop Head, just below the Kinder Plateau and were joined by ramblers from Sheffield who had come via Edale. At the end of the meeting, both groups returned the way they had come and although there had been only one earlier arrest, the Hayfield ramblers were faced with a line of police officers on their return and five more arrests were made. Following a trial at Derby Assizes, which Rothman described as an attempt to 'intimidate the ramblers' (2012, p.49), five participants received prison sentences of between one and six months and one was acquitted through lack of evidence.

Despite this outcome, mass trespasses continued in the North and spread across to other areas of the country as public interest in the campaign was further sparked. However, it was to be another six years before Arthur Creech-Jones introduced the Mountains Bill into Parliament which became what Smith (2012, p.75) regards as the 'severely emasculated and largely unused' Access to Mountains Act of 1939. Over a decade later in 1949, the National Parks and Access to the Countryside Act was passed, which allowed for access agreements with landowners, but it was still two years later that access to Kinder Scout was finally gained when the Peak District became the first National Park. In fact, over half of all the moorland and mountains that the public have access to is in the Peak District, which is surely testament to the struggles of those early ramblers.

Today, many thousands of people enjoy access to the countryside and coast as part of The Ramblers. Although not supportive of the Kinder Trespass, the Manchester Ramblers Federation had joined five other regional federations and in 1931 the National Council of Ramblers' Federations was formed to advocate at national level for walkers. In January 1935, the Ramblers' Association was officially formed and it continues to campaign today for public access as The Ramblers. Ramblers Cymru and Ramblers Scotland were subsequently formed in 1974 and 1985 respectively. Although the Ramblers had been part of the campaigning for the landmark National Parks and Access to the Countryside Act, they saw the 'right to roam' as still being illusive. In 1985, they ran the Forbidden Britain campaign for public access which was finally secured through the Countryside and Rights of Way Act (CRoW) giving public access to mountain, moor, heath and downland. This was followed by the One Coast for All campaign for secure public access to the coast in England and Wales, which contributed to the Marine and Coastal Access Act of 2009. This called on the Government to ensure footpath access to the entire coast in England, the first part of which was opened in the summer of 2012. In 2011, The Ramblers joined the widespread campaigning to stop the sale of publicly accessible woodlands by the Forestry Commission. Following increased interest in public health and well-being in 1990, The Ramblers now run various programmes aimed at increasing participation and improving the health of communities, including those in urban areas, and continue to advocate locally and nationally for the right of public access to our rich and varied national landscapes (Ramblers 2013).

The Quaker influence

The Religious Society of Friends or Quakers may not spring immediately to mind as having a prominent part to play in the traditions of using the outdoors but for many, it is the broader spirituality of open spaces that connects with us and in this sense, it is not surprising that an organisation whose tenets are simplicity, tolerance, equality and peace and who seek to experience God directly, within themselves and in their relationships with others and the world around them, should have found solitude in the great outdoors.

In his article for the *Quaker Review*, Freeman (2009) considers the influence of the Religious Society of Friends (Quakers) on the outdoors movement and the Youth Hostel Association and suggests that:

> While the outdoor activities of the Quaker renaissance were essentially internal to the Religious Society of Friends, a wider conception of social service took (them) beyond the bounds of the society in the interwar period resulting in a more profound influence on the outdoor movement. (p.1)

He goes on to note that in part, this may have resulted from the fact that many of those who promoted outdoor activity had served in the Friends Ambulance Unit (FAU) during the First World War. As pacifists, the Quakers generally believe that war and conflict serve no useful purpose and often make a situation much worse and so they are dedicated to pacifism and non-violence. The FAU was first established in 1914 and continued for the duration of the First World War. It was re-established in 1939 at the outbreak of the Second World War and its members provided post-air-raid relief, medical support, advice and welfare in Britain, and medical, hospital and ambulance crew and depot support overseas until 1946. It was replaced subsequently by the FAU Post-War Service and finally by the FAU International Service, which ceased in 1959. Freeman notes that it was this experience coupled with 'the wider horizons of a generation' that was a likely contributor to their more international outlook and interest in adventure. It is this sense of the opportunity of adventure that is shared by a number of organisations that came into being during the earlier part of the 20th century and which will be discussed later in this chapter.

The Quaker 'tramps', organised rambling events, came from the Yorkshire Quarterly Meeting where a sub-group had emerged known as the Yorkshire 1905 Committee. The tramps, the first being in the Yorkshire Dales in 1905, commemorated the death of John Wilhelm Rowntree, Quaker activist and reformer and eldest son of Joseph Rowntree the confectioner. During a speech to the 1895 Manchester Conference, he had noted that:

> No one could fail to note how swift and momentous has been the industrial revolution of the past hundred years. The creation of our great industrial classes, the massing together of men in huge centres, such as London, Birmingham and Manchester, has altered the whole fabric of society, and forces of unknown power are coming into play. (Freeman 2009)

To commemorate Willhelm, the 1905 Committee instigated the idea of the tramps and the greater spiritual experience offered by outdoor environments. It is thought that the idea of the tramps may have originated from Bootham, the Quaker school established in York in 1823. The school took the sons of the Quaker Friends, and the Rowntree family had a strong connection to it as Arthur Rowntree was Headmaster from 1899 until 1927, and both he and Arnold Rowntree had been providing Bootham boys with outdoor visits to Westmorland, which may well have provided a template for the tramps.

> In addition to walking, the trampers visited other meeting houses giving and attending lectures and although originally taking place in the Yorkshire area, they spread as far as the south west and were often combined with 'short-term residential settlement', which brought Friends

together for discussion, recreation and worship, and which served a significant educational purpose within the Society. (Freeman 2009, p.2)

This parallels the establishment of the Co-operative Holidays Association by Arthur Leonard, himself a Quaker. What may come as a surprise given that many of us today know the Quakers for their activism in the areas of peace and social witness is the somewhat militaristic structure of the tramps whereby the walkers split into small groups led by a 'captain' who was supported by a number of 'privates'. This idea of small groups or 'patrols' with an identified leader and second in command would later appear again in the Scouting movement.

Bootham School continues today as an independent school based on traditional Quaker principles and the belief that each person has within them the capacity for goodness and a responsibility to retain that goodness. Although the Quaker way is rooted in Christianity, seeing 'that of God' in everyone, the Quakers find meaning and values in the teachings of other faiths and acknowledge that the Quaker way is not the only one. Bootham School's educational philosophy is based on the idea that moral principle and a positive view of the world and its people are as important as the more traditional aspects of education philosophy. The school aims to encourage creative thinking, peacemaking and confident humanitarianism in order that its students might contribute to responsive and responsible public leadership. Among the list of past pupils are Joseph, Joshua, John Wilhelm and Benjamin Seebohm Rowntree; Phillip Noel-Baker, Olympic silver medallist and 1959 Nobel Peace Prize winner (for his work on disarmament and international peacemaking); A.J.P. Taylor, historian and left-wing campaigner; Daisy Hildyard, author of *Hunters in the Snow*; Jamie McKendrick, prize-winning modern poet; and Sophie McGill of York City Football Club.

Running through the philosophies of Octavia Hill, the Garden City movement, the struggle for public access to the countryside and the Quaker tramps is the idea that there are core conditions which are necessary for human growth and development. Our physical, mental, emotional and spiritual well-being depends on us being able to see and experience our landscapes at first hand; to breath fresh

air, to feel the sun, wind and rain on our faces, walk on the grass
and witness the passing of the seasons. Access to outdoor spaces
also provides a challenge and leads to adventure. The following
section explores the roots of some of those organisations which
provide young people with hands on experience of learning about
themselves and their ever-widening world through a connection
with natural landscapes.

The adventure spirit – young people's organisations

Perhaps the most widely known organisation for young people
is the *Scouting movement* founded for boys by Lord Baden-Powell
in 1907. Baden-Powell had been a leading figure in the siege of
Mafeking during the Boer War and had been impressed by the
initiative of a corps of boys he had put together to carry out different
supporting tasks. He saw young people as having a huge amount of
untapped potential and used his handbook for soldiers to develop a
programme for boys. In order to try out these ideas, he established
a camp in 1907 at Brownsea Island, in Poole, Dorset. The training
programme *Scouting for Boys* published in 1908, subsequently
became the handbook for the Scouting movement and by 1910,
over 100,000 young people were involved in the movement in this
country and the organisation had spread globally. In 1916, the
Wolf Cubs was started for younger scouts, and Rover Scouts for
older members commenced in 1920. As scouting developed, new
branches such as the Air and Sea Scouts were formed, supported
by the RAF and the Royal Navy, and when the Rover Scouts and
Senior Scouts were amalgamated to form the Venture Scouts, girls
were invited to join. During the 1990s, girls were also able to
access the other branches. In 1986 the Beaver Scouts was formed
for younger children aged from six to eight years old. The Scouts
retains the idea that personal challenge is crucial to a young
person's development and offers 'new challenges to enrich lives'
through a varied programme of outdoor and physical activities,
community involvement and creative expression. However, having
been created as a result of Baden-Powell's experiences during
war and having a somewhat militaristic structure with troops and

patrols, the Scouting movement was not without its critics, as will be discussed later.

Following the Scout camp at Brownsea Island, a small group of girls began scouting activities and the following year, girls attended a rally at Crystal Palace uninvited to plead with Baden-Powell to 'do something for girls too'. And so the *Girl Guide Association* was formed in 1910, led by Baden-Powell's sister Agnes. In 1914, a junior section, Rosebuds, was formed but renamed in 1915 as the Brownies, while 1916 saw the commencement of the Senior Guides for young women aged 14–25. In 1980, in recognition of the growing awareness of the important role of participation for young people, Innovate was established as a discussion group through which members' voices could contribute to the direction of guiding. 1987 saw the introduction of Rainbows for five-to seven-year-olds and in 2002, the organisation was renamed Girlguiding. As with the Scouts, its focus is challenge through adventure and outdoor activities, and it offers opportunities for creativity, fun and community involvement. One of the key aspects of Girlguiding which differentiates it from other organisations is that it has remained 'girls only' in order to give them 'a space where they can really be themselves with other girls and share the experience of growing up as a girl in today's world' (Girlguiding 2013). Although this feminist stance is a positive move today, during the post-war period, those organisations admitting both genders, such as the Woodcraft Folk, were seen as much more democratic.

It was 'Black Wolf' or Ernest Thompson Seton, wildlife illustrator, story-teller, naturalist and lecturer, who coined the term *Woodcraft*, described as a philosophy of life which stresses outdoor life and activity but also has alternative programmes for those living in urban areas and for indoor activities. Seton was born in South Shields, Durham, in 1860 moving to Canada with his parents and family in 1866. He was a supporter of the political, cultural and spiritual rights of 'first peoples', those descended from the pre-colonial and pre-invasion inhabitants of their region (First Peoples Worldwide). Seton's varied experiences included attendance on a seven-year scholarship at the Royal Academy of Art in London, authorship of numerous natural history articles, a period of study of art in Paris, hunting wolves in New Mexico, appointment as Official Naturalist to the Government of Manitoba and a 2,000-mile canoe trip in northern Canada from which he produced accurate maps used until the 1950s.

It was during 1902 that Seton published the first of a series of articles in the *Ladies Home Journal* that started the Woodcraft movement. In 1906, during a trip to England, he had met Baden-Powell who, it is claimed, subsequently used much of Seton's material and ideas for the Scouting movement, although he did not apparently credit Seton in any way. Although in 1910, Seton was chair of the founding committee of the Boy Scouts of America (serving as Chief Scout from 1910–1915), and had written their first handbook, he disliked the militaristic attitudes prevalent in the Scouting movement. They in turn disliked the Native American influence which Seton brought and so he resigned, going on to revive the Woodcraft movement through The Woodcraft League of America. Initially it was an organisation for all ages and both genders. However, the first children's organisation, the Woodcraft Rangers, was only for boys, and it was not until the 1950s that it became co-educational. The publication of his *Book of Woodcraft* in 1912 was the inspiration for many Woodcraft groups across the globe (ET Seton Institute).

The first Woodcraft Folk groups in the UK were set up in South London in 1924 and 1925, they were among the few post-war youth groups to admit both genders together. They rose out of an earlier organisation founded by John Hargrave, Quaker pacifist and leading member of the Scouts when, like Seton, he became disillusioned with a number of aspects of the Scouting tradition, not least the militaristic approach it had adopted. Having moved away from the Scouts, Hargrave started the Kindred of the Kibbo Kift (KKK), an archaic Kentish dialect phrase meaning a proof of great strength. The Kibbo Kift was open to all ages and both genders and had a core belief that an open air life would inspire those from urban areas to build a new world peace (Judge Smith).

As a result of the First World War, young people felt a sense of revulsion against conflict and the suffering it brought that was reminiscent of the Quaker pacifists. On 28 October 1920, Hargrave wrote to the Scouting movement to express his displeasure at its para-military ideas and to object to its Royal Charter and what he saw as a non-representative form of government at its headquarters. Despite having previously written for the *Scouting for Boys* handbook, he stated that it was outdated and overtly patriotic in its attitudes and he suggested that the Scouting movement should instead have been a movement for world peace (Woodcraft Folk History 2010).

Leslie Paul, born in Dublin in 1905 but brought up in south London, had also left the Scouts and joined the Kibbo Kift. In a lecture in 1985 which he gave to the Co-operative History Workshop in London he tells us that the KKK was seen by many socialists and those co-operatives affiliated directly to the Labour Party as an opportunity to unite young people in a move away from the Scouts and other similar less democratic youth movements. Paul decided to form his own KKK group and from there, to form a local organisation to bring all the south London co-operative groups together and hold an annual open-air assembly to democratically decide on policy. From here in February 1925, Paul went on to found the Wayfarers' Fellowship in Catford, the movement which led to the formation of the Woodcraft Folk (Harper).

The Woodcraft Folk describe themselves as a movement for children and young people to grow in confidence, learn about the world and start to understand how to value our planet and each other with the aim of equality, co-operation, fun and awareness of society. Their round logo depicting two trees against a rising sun symbolises democracy and the growth of young people into a new world of equality, justice and peace. The Folk receive financial support from co-operative organisations and maintain close links with other international youth organisations which share their philosophy of participation, empowerment, active citizenship and support for the welfare of children and young people. The Woodcraft Folk activities focus on camping and the outdoors. The strong tradition of democracy – the idea that it is run by children and young people for children and young people – still sets it apart from many other youth organisations, although the participation and empowerment agenda has strengthened in recent years (Woodcraft Folk History 2010). Seton's legacy is in both the use of the outdoors and the idea that we all should first find ourselves and then be with ourselves without fear.

> Woodcraft is a philosophy of life, a different approach to the outer world and a method of creating a personal inner world. (ET Seton Institute)

An awareness of society in addition to an understanding of ourselves is echoed in the philosophy of many of those groups, which continue to offer development opportunities to young people today.

Kurt Hahn, born in Germany in 1896, son of a wealthy Jewish industrialist and founder of *The Outward Bound Trust*, fled to England in 1933 under threat from the Nazis for standing up against aggression (Gordonstoun School History 2013). He was a key figure in in the promotion of experiential education, regarding its purpose to be to ensure the survival of enterprising curiosity, an undefeatable spirit, tenacity in pursuit, readiness for sensible self-denial and, above all, compassion. He based his philosophy on the idea that young people had the potential to develop both personally and as part of a community, and having been Head of the Salem School in Germany which was based on experiential learning, service to the community and the participation of the pupils in the running of the school, once in Britain, he set up Gordonstoun School in 1934 (Round Square 2012).

Lawrence Holt was a senior partner in the Liverpool-based Blue Funnel Shipping Line. He was interested in Hahn's philosophy and the programme he ran at Gordonstoun and asked him to provide a short residential course for his then 'County Badge' scheme which later became the Duke of Edinburgh's Award scheme. Out of his partnership with Hahn emerged the first Outward Bound School in Aberdovey, Wales. The school offered many outdoor pursuits, including boat handling and survival skills, which served to meet the needs of Holt's cadet merchant seaman and also what he saw as the youth of a nation at war who were not prepared for the uncertain future. This philosophy, which recognises that through outdoor challenges, young people can become more independent, self-aware, able to cope for themselves and build physical and emotional resilience, resonates strongly with that of the Forest Movement (Outward Bound).

Gordonstoun School retains the philosophy of Hahn and bases its approach on four key principles of challenge, service, internationalism and responsibility. As opposed to simple instruction, it offers experiential learning through expedition, adventure and seamanship and addresses the academic, physical and emotional needs of the students to prepare them for international citizenship. Hahn's legacy through Gordonstoun is the Round Square, a worldwide association of schools sharing a commitment to his philosophy. The Pillars of the Round Square incorporate a set of core principles which embrace political, social and economic ideals such as democracy, justice, international tolerance and understanding, environmental stewardship and service to others. Although a fee-paying independent school, in order to give wider access, Gordonstoun offers bursaries and scholarship places which support over 25 per cent of the students.

Today, the Duke of Edinburgh's Award has charitable status and continues to offer young people from all walks of life opportunities for developing their full potential through programmes which are designed to support the growth of the whole person – mind, body and soul – and to develop self-confidence and self-esteem.

The original *Forest School* was started in 1929 and although similar in approach to the more recent Forest School movement, it came from very different roots. Ernest Westlake, co-founder of the Order of Woodcraft Chivalry, had acquired land at Godshill on the edge of the New Forest. He wanted to set up a Forest School based on Quaker principles to enable children to develop independence in an outdoor environment (Institute of Education 2009). The school ran on its original site until 1938 when it was relocated to Whitwell Hall in Norfolk but at the outbreak of the Second World War, the Hall was requisitioned for military use and the school did not reopen. In 1947, members of the school staff decided to continue with the ideals of Forest School by establishing *Forest School Camp*, again in the New Forest, based on Woodcraft principles. The popularity of the camps increased in the 1950s, through interest from parents who were more left wing and seeking alternative experiences for their children.

Today, Forest School Camps is a registered educational charity, staffed by volunteers. Its philosophy is based on the Woodcraft movement, progressive education principles and Native American, Quaker and other similar ideals. The camps provide experience for children to learn and play together with the adult volunteers while being close to nature. As with the other organisations discussed in this chapter, the camps aim to promote independence and encourage children to take responsibility for themselves and their actions, to develop concern, tolerance and respect for others and to act responsibly towards the environment (About Forest School Camps 2013).

At the time of the first Forest School and in response to the high number of unemployed men, a new 'community' camp was set up in the New Forest named Grith Fyrd or Peace Army. Although it was based on army traditions of self-discipline, self-control, *espirit de corps* and physical fitness, the aim was to apply these instead to a lifetime of peaceful and communal service. The majority of those who attended the first camp were unemployed and this opportunity was seen as a call to adventure. In the heart of nature they learned life lessons away from the rush of the everyday world. The camp was self-sufficient and the men made shelters, learning to cut timber and to thatch, grow vegetables and spin and weave fabric for clothing. Leisure activities were based around leathercraft, woodcarving, painting, pottery and dancing. Sometimes they would join with the Forest School Camp for visits to the cinema or folk dancing. They were also able to study with the Workers' Educational Association by wireless so that both mental and physical well-being were attended to.

Although there are some unique differences in each of these organisations, what unites them is a recognition that in order to develop their full potential, children and young people need to be in the outdoors. They need to be active participants in their learning and leisure and to be challenged physically, mentally and emotionally in a supportive environment where they are respected and valued. In this way, they develop confidence and self-belief, learn how to work together, develop compassion and tolerance for others and understand how they fit into both their local and global communities. It is this democratic approach which also links with what is known as the progressive education movement.

The 'progressive' educators

It is beyond the scope of this book to cover the whole span of progressive education but the approach in general is consistent with many of the principles of the above organisations. Rather than focusing on curriculum content, progressive education is concerned with the child's processes of learning. Key concepts are child-centred, democratic education and social constructivism. The first child-centred schools in Britain opened in the late 19th and early 20th centuries in what is known as 'the New Education movement' and many of the headteachers of progressive schools were associated with the New Educational Fellowship, founded in 1921. Perhaps some of the best known names of such educators are Friedrich Froebel, John Dewey, Rudolph Steiner and Maria Montessori.

Froebel, a German educationalist born in 1782, is best known for the idea of 'kindergartens'. Far from just being a school for small children, kindergarten refers to the idea of a garden for children and of children, originating from the first kindergarten that Froebel established in Bad Blankenburg as a protection for children from industrialisation. At the rear of the building was a plot of land where each child had their own tiny garden. As a child, Froebel had what might be described today as a 'free range' childhood. His mother had died and his father, who was a pastor, had left him largely to occupy himself, which he did through developing a love of nature and a strong Christian faith.

From the experience in his first teaching position, he was also influenced by the approach of Johann Pestalozzi, a Swiss educationalist who believed, like many of those above, that the divisions within society could be healed by education of the whole person: their head, their hands and their heart. The key to Froebel's approach was his recognition that play is central to the child's learning and in play, children connect up biological processes with the socio-cultural (Bruce 2011). To assist the child's explorations, he developed a set of wooden blocks and small balls, similar to the wooden building blocks we see today. He recognised that all learners are productive and creative and developed the idea of learning being promoted through the use of 'gifts' or play materials used in 'occupations' or activities. Froebel was the first educator to understand the importance of high-quality educational experiences from birth to seven but also to recognise our lifelong potential for learning, both of which are crucial aspects of current educational thinking.

Although *John Dewey*, an American educationalist, is generally considered in the context of child-centred education, he also recognised the importance of gaining an understanding of children's personal experiences and of accepting their uniqueness, which he saw as both genetically and experientially determined. However, contrary to popular belief, he was not an advocate of free, democratically led education but believed that children learned best when supported and directed in structuring their own learning. Gray and Macblain (2012) note two key aspects of Dewey's thinking. First, that schools should be seen as communities, and second, that although the child's past experience can affect how they might learn, teachers need to work in the present and the future, rather than using the past to limit their view of what a child can do. They also highlight Dewey's view that education should prepare children to be effective participants within society and that those societies need to value their children and the contributions they can make.

Maria Montessori was the first woman in Italy to study medicine and her interest in education arose out of her contact with children in the asylums of Rome and her subsequent directorship of a medical-pedagogical institute for 'retarded' children. Following this she established the first Casa dei Bambini in 1907 to cater for the youngest children of migrant workers who would otherwise have been left to roam the streets while their parents were at work (Isaacs 2007). As with Dewey, Montessori recognised and celebrated the underlying potential and uniqueness of each child and suggested three key components in her method of education: the child, the environment and the teacher. Since she considered it crucial for children to take responsibility for their own learning, she recognised the need for appropriate child-sized furniture for the Casa dei Bambini, which she then designed herself. Attention to the physical environment in which children learn has continued to be an important aspect of current practice at all levels of education.

A key feature of Montessori's approach was the idea of 'planes' or 'stages' which are passed through as children's learning develops. The first plane is seen as the primary learning area when the most significant changes are seen in physical, social and emotional development, changes which are crucial to later development and which are encompassed in the discussion in Chapter 3. Montessori also understood the importance of sensory learning, although as Gray and Macblain (2012) note, she did not give much importance to imaginary play, but instead preferred children to engage in practical activities which were based on real situations the children were part of, such as keeping their shared space ordered instead of pretending to play schools. However, her approach identified the child's innate drive to undertake practical, experiential activities involving all their senses without paying any mind to whether they constituted work or play. Her ideas continue to influence practice today, with 600 schools in the UK, over 4,000 in the USA and a network of others worldwide.

Those parents who are disillusioned with the education offered in mainstream state schools today may opt to send their children to a Steiner school, based on the philosophy of *Rudolph Steiner*, which promises to 'honour and protect the wonder of childhood' (Knight 2009 p.62). Steiner was an innovative Austrian academic who believed that education should foster a love of learning and develop the whole child, physically, socially, emotionally, intellectually, culturally and spiritually. He opened his first school in Stuttgart in response to a request from the owner of the Waldorf Astoria cigarette factory who wanted a school for the children of his workers. Today there are over 1,000 Steiner schools worldwide and over 2,000 early years establishments (Gray and Macblain 2012, p.23). Steiner recognised the importance of children developing a strong sense of self and diverse capacities that enable them to become socially and economically responsible citizens. Steiner education today aims to promote universal values, educational pluralism and meaningful teaching and learning opportunities and recognises the importance of a curriculum which can work in harmony with the different developmental phases children pass through. There is an emphasis on an unhurried, creative learning environment and a balance between practical, artistic and intellectual activities in order to produce well-balanced and rounded individuals who can cope with a fast-changing world. All Steiner schools are co-educational, fully comprehensive and multi-faith.

Developing a personal philosophy

It was the work of Carl Rogers, along with my experience at an outdoor education centre which inspired me to reconsider my own teaching approach. In the introduction to his book *Freedom to Learn for the 80's* (1983, p.3), Rogers notes that he aims to guide teachers towards an awareness that the good life is within and not dependent on outside sources. He also offers us the idea of creating a climate of trust within the classroom to nourish the students' natural curiosity to learn and developing a more democratic, participatory mode of decision making in all parts of the school. He cites the German philosopher Heidegger who noted that 'Teaching is more difficult than learning because what teaching calls for is this: to let learn… let nothing else be learned than – learning' (p.18).

This idea of standing back, of being a facilitator for the child's natural curiosity to learn and to understand the world around them is, I think, particularly significant today when so much of children's time and activity is conceived, directed and controlled by adults. When I later decided to train as a play therapist, I chose a Rogerian perspective which acknowledges that the child can be the architect of their own healing if the right core conditions are created.

Several years after qualifying and living in Somerset, I came across the *Forest School Movement*, started by staff from Bridgwater College near where I worked, following a trip to Denmark in 1994 with their early years students. This way of working with children in outdoor environments had developed in Denmark in the 1950s but is now widely used throughout Scandinavia and is based on the tradition of being close to nature.

At this time I was working as a specialist practitioner for pupils with social, emotional and behavioural difficulties (SEBD) and growing increasingly frustrated at the lack of therapeutic opportunities for children who had complex SEBD. Knight (2009) tells of her growing concern that many children are hustled through the first crucial years of education from birth to seven by a formal system which sets great store by conformity to predetermined classroom behaviours. There seemed to be limited opportunity for exploratory learning at a pace which suited the child's development, and many of those children I worked with were being excluded from school because they couldn't conform to these predetermined expectations which took little account of life experiences or the stage of development they were at. There was also little recognition that if what had already been offered had failed them, doing yet more of the same old things was really not going to help. Forest School, with its emphasis on developing the whole child thorough relationship-based, child-led learning opportunities in the outdoors seemed to me to have much to offer. I found the key elements of its approach to be very similar to Axline's (1967) principles of play therapy and I began to see a potential for a different therapeutic provision that combined the two approaches by taking play therapy into outdoor environments.

Axline's principles (1967)

- The therapist must develop a warm, friendly relationship with the child, in which good rapport is established as soon as possible.

- The therapist accepts the child exactly as she is.

- The therapist establishes a feeling of permissiveness in the relationship so that the child feels free to express her feelings completely.

- The therapist is alert to the *feelings* the child is expressing and reflects those feelings back to her in such a way that she gains insight into her behaviour.

- The therapist maintains a deep respect for the child's ability to solve her own problems if given the opportunity to do so. The responsibility to make choices and institute change is the child's.

- The therapist does not attempt to direct the child's actions or conversations in any way. The child leads the way; the therapist follows.

- The therapist does not attempt to hurry the therapy along. It is a gradual process and is recognised as such by the therapist.

- The therapist establishes only those limitations that are necessary to anchor the therapy to the world of reality and to make the child aware of her responsibility in the relationship.

Forest School elements (Knight 2009)

- Trust is central.

- There is no such thing as bad weather, only bad clothing.

- The setting is not the usual one.

- Forest School's holistic approach develops intellectual, emotional, physical, creative and spiritual potential.

- The learning is play based and as far as possible, child-initiated and child-led.

- The staff are trained.

- Forest School happens over time.

- The blocks and sessions have beginnings and ends.

- The Forest School is made as safe as is reasonably possible in order to facilitate the children's risk taking.

At this time, I also came across the Reggio Emilia approach used by a number of early years settings which is based on the philosophy of Loris Malaguzzi who himself was influenced by the social constructivism of Lev Vygotsky. Reggio Emilia is a northern Italian town which has become internationally renowned for its community supported system of early childhood education and care. Malaguzzi believed that in a new post-war society, children should be seen as able to act and think for themselves. There is no written Reggio Emilia curriculum but a belief that children learn to co-construct their theories and knowledge through relationships with others and their environments underpinned by a set of guiding principles. It was these that I felt resonated with the process of play therapy, particularly:

- The environment is the third teacher.

- The adult is mentor and guide.

- Children have a hundred 'languages'.

It was the first of these that gave me the idea of what I now refer to as the 'nature mother', the third element in the process. The idea of the adult as mentor and guide sits comfortably, I feel, with the role of the play therapist, and the hundred languages of children are the myriad ways they have of expressing themselves non-verbally through the play, painting, dancing, making music, sculpture, through mess and chaos and all other forms of creative activities. Since embarking on therapy in the outdoors, I have become familiar with other similar modes of working, and aspects of each, both consciously and unconsciously, have informed my practice.

Nature Nurture is based in Aberdeen and does work with children from 0–16 to promote resilience and tackle vulnerability. The programme of 20 sessions combines free play and nurturing interactions in natural environments so that children can play, create, explore, socialise and challenge themselves with the support of attuned and specially trained adults. Many of those they work with come from families where there is alcohol abuse, drug misuse or domestic violence and these children face challenges at home, in school and within their communities as a result. One of the key aims is to break the generational cycle of neglect and abuse and so improve life chances for vulnerable young people (Nature Nurture 2011).

The Wilderness Foundation was started in 1974 by Sir Laurens van der Post, writer, explorer and philosopher and Dr Ian Player DMS, renowned for saving the white rhino. The foundation offers opportunities to children, young people and adults to experience the outdoors through a number of projects aimed at self-development, taking personal responsibility and increasing life opportunities. The philosophy of the foundation is that our wild spaces have an irreplaceable value, contain the wonders of pristine nature and enable us to return to our origins and draw on a deep sense of belonging and inspiration. The emblem of the Erithrina leaf symbolises three key relationships: person to divinity, person to person and person to soil, with a fourth relationship being the internal relationship we each have with ourselves (Wilderness Foundation UK 2012).

Nature therapy is a creative approach that takes place in nature and considers nature as a partner in the therapeutic process. It is the integration of a number of approaches, including expressive arts therapy, gestalt, ecopsychology and adventure therapy (Berger and Lahad 2013, Nature Therapy Center 2010). It relates to the bond between human beings and nature and the use of the healing power of nature to promote and expand the existing therapeutic process. Nature therefore becomes a partner in the process. Berger and Lahad discuss the Therapeutic Triangle, which they tell us is a central term in nature therapy and is based on the traditional dyadic relationship between therapist and client but introduces the third element of nature. The facilitator is then free either to 'increase interaction with the client with nature as a back drop or supplier of materials or adopt a more passive role as facilitator between the client and nature' (p.44). In this way, they suggest, both transpersonal and inter-personal work can take place. Nature therapy also recognises the traditional idea that, over time, communities across the globe developed rituals to help both individuals and groups cope with uncertainty and transitions, many of which were linked to nature. These were handed down from generation to generation but our more recent societal move towards more isolated living and our disconnection from the land has left us depleted.

The ecopsychology movement recognises that:

> Climate change, ecological and economic crisis, as well as social unrest, are all signs that our planet is in great distress. We humans are being called to wake up, dramatically, to our physical as well as our psychological interconnectedness with other-than-human species and with the more-than-human world. (Ecopsychology 2013)

The field of ecopsychology is a developing one which seeks to understand ways of increasing the emotional connection between individuals and the natural world. In this way, we can learn how to live sustainable lives which respect nature and rebuild our connection to that which provided for us but which we have come to take for granted. As with nature therapy, this approach is more than psychotherapy done outdoors. It has at its centre the idea of the ecological 'self', the concept of our own identity being in and of nature from our very beginnings:

The meaning of life, the joy we experience in living is enhanced through increased self-realization, that is through fulfilment of potentials that each of us has…that are never the same for any two human beings…increased self-realization implies a broadening and deepening of the self. (Naess 2008)

In taking my play therapy practice into the outdoors, it is this increased self-realisation which I believe my clients can access through the development of a healthy body self – a deeper knowing of their very visceral physicality – and by establishing an attachment with the 'nature mother' that recognises our interdependence and can sustain them into the future (see Chapter 3).

Chapter 2

A Current Context for Childhood

This chapter will explore the current social culture which informs adults' views of children and children's views of themselves and consider some of the major influences in this relationship. It will discuss changes to children's leisure activities in recent times and give a current context for children growing up. It will look at the role the outdoors has had in children's play, how this has changed and some of the problems which may have arisen as a result of this change. It will include some definitions of play and position non-directive play therapy in the outdoors as a counter balance to the fractured relationship between children and nature and as a way of developing a secture sense of body self.

The true measure of a nation's standing is how well it attends to its children – their health and safety, their material security, their education and socialization, and their sense of being loved, valued, and included in the families and societies into which they are born. (UNICEF 2007, p.1)

There is a complex and intertwining relationship between how society views children and resulting government policies. Our cultural representations of young people, how we engage with them, the influence of the media through reporting, portrayal in films, adverts and on television and the resulting persistent stereotyping all have a significant impact on the views that shape policy. Yet what is so often missing is young people's own voices so that our misperceptions of the issues they face shape a popular but often ill-conceived idea of what it is like to be growing up in this country today. While it is beyond the scope of this book to provide a detailed discourse on childhood, it is important to look at those issues which the adult world sees as impacting on childhood, since these cultural perceptions heavily influence most aspects of their lives. Any discussion of current culture must also recognise that implicit in this term is a recognition that our society is made up of a diverse and rich mixture of cultural heritages and each of these may view childhood and parental responsibility differently.

Defining childhood

For the purposes of this book, childhood may be said to span the years between 0 and 19, although perhaps after 16 any cut-off point could be said to be arbitrary since we do not grow, develop or mature at the same rate and our life experiences can be vastly different. We might have viewed the post-16 years as the beginning of the transition to adulthood but 2013 saw the first cohort of secondary school children who will remain in full-time education or training until they are 18 and so our understanding of childhood may again be challenged. It is also important that we have a common understanding of the terms we use to describe the 0–19 age group. I feel it is crucial that we use the term 'children' in order to continue to recognise our responsibility towards guiding them to adulthood, although accepting that as they head towards their middle years between 8 and 14, they develop their understanding of the complexities of life, allowing them to become more discerning participants in society. However, the term 'young people' is equally important in both meaning and usage. We need to use it to remind ourselves that they are indeed young people and should be accorded those rights and privileges we accord ourselves as adults, but with the recognition again that they are young and therefore may make mistakes as we all do and still need nurture, sensitive guidance and above all respect which acknowledges their growing independence and autonomy. Within this book I often use 'children' when I am specifically referring to those under 11, and 'young people' to refer to those over that age but I also use the terms interchangeably in order to hold on to the two concepts above.

If I look back to my childhood and compare it with my children's experience, there are obvious differences but also similarities. I lived in a small rural town in Wiltshire, spent my first 11 years growing up in a council house with a large garden, had access to fields and the surrounding streets and was part of a large group of children who 'hung out' together, in various combinations for most of the time. We didn't tend to sleep over at each other's houses but had numerous birthday parties catered for by our parents which took place at home. Friends were dropped off and collected but their parents didn't stay and we played party games such as pin the tail on the donkey, blind man's buff, musical chairs and pass the parcel. My parents didn't spend social time with my friends' parents and when we went out and about, it was to the playing fields, occasionally to each other's houses, across the fields and around the streets on our bikes. Our games were the more traditional chasing and hiding games, building dens and playing in the stream or at home, colouring, creative crafts, jigsaws and board games. I had dolls, a cot and pram and a doll's house which my father made for me to play with and, around the age of seven, a Sindy doll whose clothes were 'respectable': a riding outfit, a country ensemble consisting of slacks, a suede coat and a headscarf, and evening attire consisting of a long dress and gloves. Other outfits were made by my aunty, such as cardigans and twinsets and neat woollen skirts! We were among the last houses in the street to get a television and I don't recall that we had a private phone, although there was a public telephone box just down the road. We did have a car. For most of my primary years, I went to the same school that my parents taught at and I travelled with them by car. During what is now Year 6 I went to the 'local' primary, still well over a mile away, and either walked there or went on the bus with my friends. It was not until I started secondary school that my parents could afford to move into a private house on an established estate at the other end of town. From here I caught the bus to the girls' high school I attended in a nearby town as a result of having passed the 11-plus. We holidayed in the same caravan in Cornwall until I was in my teens when my mother and I ventured abroad to visit my brother and his family.

My own children grew up for the most part in a small rural town in Somerset in a modest Edwardian terraced house which we owned. It had a long garden and was close to a park but access to the fields was some distance away and therefore fields were not an immediate playground for them. We had a television and video player, a private phone, our own car and a VW camper van. They knew the children that lived close by and with whom they went to school and they also had friends who were the children of our friends – the ones with whom we socialised. They played chase and hide and seek around the house and garden and sometimes in the park, had board games, art materials, books and jigsaws and were generally creative, both indoors and outside. They went to child-minders and had sleep-overs and as they grew up, the distance they ventured from the house increased. We went to different places for our holidays, often with friends and often abroad and took the children to music festivals. Branded goods were on the rise, with McDonald's, Pizza Hut, Coke, Pepsi, Nike, Ellesse and the like, and there was a limited degree of what has become known as 'pester power' which I have to say we resisted for the most part! By the time they went to secondary school, we also had a computer, the internet and a mobile phone.

Within that one generational jump, considering that my parents had similar 'professional' jobs, we seemed to have considerably more disposable income than they had had at a similar stage in their life and the number of 'things' – material possessions – we owned had significantly increased. Television adverts for children's toys were very stereotyped and advertised numerous 'branded' items, encouraging boys towards action toys, with dark colours and deeply masculine and aggressive voiceovers, often tinged with an American accent, while girls toys were predominantly pink and purple and aimed at getting them to take on a caring role of some sort or to experiment with 'fashion' – hair styles, make-up and clothes – either personally or through dolls such a Barbie.

Come forward another generation and Varney and Beder (2009, p.23) note that, '(one) of the phrases of Teen Talk Barbie is "Let's go shopping!"' which they suggest sums up 'the cross promotion and the celebration of rampant consumerism, leaving questions of children's development and meaningful play forgotten in their wake'. The commercialisation of childhood appears to be one of four major issues repeatedly highlighted in the media as facing parents and wider society today, the others being an increase in sexualised or 'pornified' material which children can be exposed to in a variety of settings, the increase in the availability and use of technology in the form of games, television and social networking and access to an ever-expanding worldwide web, coupled with a decrease in access to outdoor play spaces and a contrasting diminishing of children's real worlds.

Buying our children's loyalty

As part of the Government's 2009 report *The Importance of the Commercial World on Children's Wellbeing*, Loughborough University's Centre for Research in Social Policy and Department of Social Science looked at the marketing and advertising industries' strategies towards children and young people. The authors noted that whereas once upon a time, play was going outside, now it tends to involve 'commercial products such as games consoles' but they also argue that there are two contrasting perspectives on commercialisation. The first would suggest that the commercial world is part of everyday reality and children should engage with it and learn from it since they are quite capable of making their own judgements about products and advertising without strict legislation. The second would suggest that children's learning and development require a multi-faceted space, and relentless exposure to commercial messages erodes this space (France 2010). The child-focused advertising market in the UK has been worth around £30 billion pounds and children in the UK, US and Australia can be exposed to up to 20,000–40,000 TV advertisements a year. In addition, there is advertising on public transport, at sports grounds and leisure centres, on clothing and even in education settings through the various supermarket-backed voucher schemes to 'buy' computers, sports equipment and gardening products. However, France (2010) concludes that there is still only weak evidence of the impact of commercialisation on overall child well-being so we might therefore suppose that the somewhat polarised current public debate is merely an emotive response to a changing world. But even if there is weak evidence of negative effects of increased commercialisation, perhaps there is an ethical stance that we might take when schools in the UK are targeted by brands to the tune of £300 million and schools in the US, underfunded by government, receive around $2.5 million from commercial corporations, ensuring that brand names are embedded in children's minds from a very early age (Beder, Varney and Gosden 2008, Drauglis 2003, Molnar 2005). It may well be the case that children and young people are neither passive victims of advertising nor entirely discerning and astute consumers and although most will develop the capacity to understand marketing techniques as they move into secondary education, adult and parental guidance is needed, particularly in their formative years, and many of us will see the use of schools as vast advertising hoardings as an undesirable facet of increased commercialisation.

I noted in the introduction to this book that rose-tinted spectacles are a great advantage in retrospection but the commercial world has had at least a toe in the water of education for decades. I can remember sending away for labels and posters from a range of food companies both as a child and in my early teaching days but the specific targeting of schools does appear to have increased significantly over the last 20 years. So, although I do not in any way think there was necessarily a 'golden age' of childhood, I do note that the reality of today's society is that it seems much more materialistic than when I was growing up.

It can appear that many parents equate buying a child something with evidence of their care for that child and my own observations over 30+ years of working with children and families is that there is also a significant change in the nature of the relationship which many parents have with their children – a shift from authoritative parenting which understands the need for boundaries, respectful child-centred relationships, good communication and the fostering of play and creativity to a need to treat children as some kind of small adult, exposing them to ideas, material possessions and media influences way beyond their years. I think we have an interesting and somewhat bizarre attitude to children within our social culture and although a fuller discussion of childhood today is beyond the scope of this book, it is important to look at the changes in how society views it in order to set the context for the relational paradigm of play therapy.

Sexualisation – the promotion of gender stereotypes

Last year the Mail Online (Saunders 2013) featured an article about model Heidi Klum and her daughter which ran with the headline, 'Model in the making! Heidi Klum's daughter Leni looks every inch her mother's mini-me with matching glasses, scarf and bag.' The article noted that:

> It's little wonder Heidi Klum's adorable daughter Leni seems to be following in her footsteps. Proving that she has become quite the fashionista of late, the eight-year-old youngster seemed to have imitated her mother's sense of style as the family stepped out for a bite to eat on Wednesday lunchtime.

The accompanying photo showed the eight-year-old dressed in 'a white lace overlay dress, black boots and a heart-motif knitted jumper…with a chic monochrome scarf and a pair of black aviator sunglasses', clothing which was described as a 'daytime ensemble', hardly the language used to describe the average children's outfit. The use of the word imitate is also interesting. Children have always played 'dressing up', and imitating adults through role play is how we learn about the world. But there is a difference between imitating them in a childlike way and becoming constructed carbon copies. An ensemble so exactly matching as the one describe above would seem to require the parent to be involved in the purchasing of it, a far cry from bridal wear made from old net curtains, superhero capes made from towels, and knights' helmets and shields made from cardboard boxes. In another article, they had photographed the same child coming out of a gym class and described her as a 'leggy beauty', a comment for which they were heavily criticised by their readers.

While we might all share a somewhat horrified view of this kind of sexualisation of young children by the press, it does also beg the question of why some parents might feel the need to dress their children in their own likeness rather than letting them develop their own more age-appropriate style. Although there may a broad but shared understanding of the term commercialisation, there is no similar shared definition for sexualisation and perceptions of what is sexualised and what isn't are likely to vary quite considerably, particularly between adults and young people. Buckingham (2011) cites language as an example of this and suggests that although young people's language may appear overtly sexualised, their meaning is both complex and dynamic and they are likely to be unaware of the original linguistic meanings which adults hold.

The obvious increase in sexualised advertising and images which now proliferate our public spaces, screens, newspapers and magazines is widely recognised but as with commercialisation, the evidence of its negative impact is sparse and once again opinions tend to be polarised. Yet despite the lack of hard evidence, there are consequences such as those noted by Gill (2011), who reports that research among what were described as 'tweenage' girls found that although they might feel able to deconstruct sexualised images, they also experience negative feelings in response to them and feel pressured by them. Perhaps one of the more concerning aspects of the prevalence of sexualised imagery is that it has a tendency to normalise gender stereotyping so girls continue to be seen as sexually available and boys as dominant and having a high degree of sexual prowess. Coy (2011) suggests that girls need an alternative view of their bodies which is based on their full capabilities and potential, rather than a sexualised ideal, but feels that this also needs to be supported by a more equal representation of women in terms of socio-economic position and representation in political decision making. She sees this as crucial to a more healthy holistic development of girls' self-image and I would suggest that a healthier view of their bodies is also necessary for boys.

Concerns over access to pornography, either sought out or encountered incidentally, and the use of social networks to circulate sexualised images both self-generated and those encountered on websites seem to be growing and are certainly of current interest in the media. Much comment is concerned with the stereotypical and unreal appearance and roles of those involved in commercially produced images and the impact this has on young people's perceptions of what is normal within sexual relationships. Adolescence is a time of curiosity and investigation about our developing and future sexual selves and sexual relationships. In the past, young people might well have accessed material from books, magazines and films but with the internet, wider access to more disturbing images is easier and ideas of what is normal are becoming skewed. A survey of 18–24-year-olds conducted by Vodafone and BBC Radio 1 in 2011 found that 71 per cent of those surveyed thought that access to pornography was too easy, 50 per cent felt it could make you feel bad about yourself and 63 per cent thought it could be harmful to ideas about sex and sexuality (Wood 2013).

Popular culture suggests that some young men on encountering young women with pubic hair are alarmed at the sight since many of the women in pornographic images have little or none at all. Girls may well, by the same token, see men as dominant and their own role as submissive or themselves as passive participants in a range of sometimes extreme and/or violent sexual acts. This type of portrayal of abuse and degradation of women is likely to be more harmful then just the sexualised nature of the material. Research carried out by Livingstone *et al.* and UK Kids Online (2013) suggests that 22 per cent of the 10,000 young people surveyed were concerned about pornography online and 18 per cent by violence. They also point out that violence is of greater concern to boys and suggest it receives much less public attention, although many children are concerned 'about violent, aggressive or gory online content. They reveal shock and disgust on seeing cruelty, killings, abuse of animals and even the news – since much of it is real rather than fictional violence, this adds to the depth of children's reactions' (p.1). So here again, adult perceptions of what causes concerns among young people appear to be wide of the mark.

The need for authoritative parenting

To underline this, sexualised and gender-stereotyped clothing, products and services were the biggest cause for concern from parents and non-commercial organisations surveyed for the Government's report of the independent review of the commercialisation and sexualisation of childhood, with scaled down versions of adult clothing, suggestive slogans and gender stereotyping through colour cited in particular (Bailey 2011). The report did, however, note that views relating to the suitability of clothes are subjective and need to take account of differing ideas of what constitutes 'good taste', availability, cost and individual choice. Yet, in contrast to this, Buckingham (2011) notes that research for the Scottish Parliament found that the sexualised goods were low on parents' lists of priorities and the that the current public outrage did not reflect the real perceptions about sexualised goods of either children or parents. He highlights the fact that parents felt children had a right to develop and express themselves individually and so for some, copying 'sexy' dancing was innocuous and devoid of adult sexual connotations, yet for others it will be seen as distasteful. It may be that more worrying than children copying sexualised dancing is that such images have come to be seen by some as normal behaviour. Simply to say that there is no conclusive evidence to say something is harmful, does not mean that harm is not done by it. Such is the growing public concern about commercialisation, sexualisation and the impact of increased and, in some cases, unregulated access to technological devices that in recent years there has been a number of related government reports (Byron 2008 and 2010, Bailey 2011), the latter commissioned to support the Coalition Government's 2010 commitment to tackle the commercialisation and sexualisation of childhood. The 2011 report, appropriately entitled *Letting Children Be Children* notes that:

> Parents recognise that they should be the ones to set the standards that their children live by, but in some things they need more support. In particular, parents need businesses and others to work with them and not against them. However, parents also need to accept the challenge to them and recognise that for children to be children, parents need to be parents. (Bailey 2011, p.3)

This is perhaps then one of the crucial issues for our time; that the roles of parent and child have in some cases become rather blurred and we need to restore clarity to the idea that parents need to parent and children need to be allowed to be children. This is not to infantalise children, to keep them innocent and 'done to' by adults. We need to recognise their potential ability to be discriminating consumers but not expect them to be so independently from their earliest days or at too young an age.

In my work with parents and children together this idea that parents are in charge, that their 'job' is to keep children safe without denying them independence of thought and action has often been the first area of concern we have had to address. It is undoubtedly a complex issue which needs to take many factors into account, not least parents' own histories of being parented, but it is frequently the crucial factor in restoring equilibrium where there is conflict within family relationships. In raising this, I am not seeking to blame parents for capitulating to children's demands or for wanting their children to have whatever it appears is needed in order for them to feel included with their peers. The very nature of a capitalist economy such as ours is the distorted relationship between what we know as supply and demand. The demand is largely created by a vast advertising industry, backed by consumer psychology which creates 'lifestyles' for all ages designed to make us feel happier, healthier, accepted and more successful and thereby tapping in to our collective insecurities. This creates a supply of material goods which we have then supposedly demanded. But it is profit and not our well-being that that drives commercialism.

The idea that children are just another consumer group to be exploited seems at odds with the prevailing societal idea that they are somehow 'victims' in the making, constantly vulnerable and at continuous risk from a wide variety of factors, from alcohol consumption to obesity, from sexual predators to bullies in the playground and from traffic on the roads to pollution of the environment. However, against this we can situate the alternate view which often prevails through the breadth of media sources, that young people are the devil incarnate, anti-social in their habits and aggressive and uncompromising in their attitudes and behaviour. On the one hand, our society seems to want to protect children from perceived danger to the extent that many parents will not let their children out of their sight and there are dozens of initiatives and programmes to encourage our children to become healthier, fitter and more aware of danger, and on the other hand, they are seen as an exploitable commodity by advertisers and commercial companies. And herein lies a paradox – that millions of pounds of taxpayers' money is spent on healthy living programmes to tackle the effect of poor diet and lack of exercise, often a result of consumption of highly advertised 'junk' food, and the promotion of screen-focused leisure and play activities. What kind of mixed messages are we sending our children when schools are teaching e-safety to protect them from unsuitable internet material but the 'opt in' system of access to adult websites is furiously resisted by internet providers and funding for the Child Exploitation and Online Protection Service (CEOPS) is cut? As I write this, there is a case in the news of a 17-year-old boy who is said to have taken his own life as a result of an online blackmailing scam. He reportedly thought he was talking to a young American girl but the presumably explicit conversation on Skype was recorded and he was threatened with circulation of the images unless he paid up (*The Guardian* 2013).

All this of course comes with a health warning itself in that without significant personal research, detailed information for all of us is often limited to what can be read in the papers or accessed via the radio, television and internet. That is why it is crucial that the construct of both childhood and adolescence in our society is authentic and that we do not just rely on a narrow range of media sources which each have their own bias. A Mori poll carried out in 2005 and published in *Young People Now* magazine looked at whether the tone of their media coverage had changed between 2004 and 2005. Although there had been a drop in negative commentary from 71 per cent to 57 per cent, there was not a corresponding rise in positivity. Instead, there was an increase of the same proportion in the amount of neutral coverage which it was suggested left readers with a more balanced if somewhat ambiguous view of young people. As a society, we appear to be unable to affirm our young people and one might wonder what would be different if we did.

Understanding well-being

In 2009, Layard and Dunn reported on children's experiences of childhood for The Children's Society in *A Good Childhood: Searching for Values in a Competitive Age*. They noted that although for children today there are better health prospects, more educational opportunities, increased self-knowledge and a greater appreciation of diversity, there are also a number of issues which are cause for concern for both adults and young people themselves relating to the issues of commercial pressure, as has already been noted above, violence and a more stressful education system which will be discussed later. All of this appears to be underpinned by a decrease in levels of happiness and an increase in what might be termed 'emotional distress' (or decreased well-being).

Here we would do well to consider the term 'well-being' since our individual understandings of it may differ. The Department for Children, Schools and Families (DCFS) recognised it as a broad and contested term and suggest in popular usage it is considered to be 'equivalent to happiness or feeling good' but note also that it has 'important social and economic dimensions' in which children are regarded as active participants in, and contributors to, society' (DCFS/DCMS 2009, p.19). Further to this, it notes that this definition goes beyond the notion of good mental health and encompasses the five key areas outlined in the Children Act of 2004:

- physical and mental health and emotional well-being

- protection from harm and neglect

- education, training and recreation

- the contribution made by young people to society

- social and economic well-being.

These in turn translate into the five outcomes from Every Child Matters (2005).

An earlier report released by the United Nations International Children's Emergency Fund (UNICEF) in 2007, which focused on child well-being in 21 rich countries (not including Australia and New Zealand), notes that the concept of well-being must start with the United Nations Convention on the Rights of the Child and in particular articles 24 and 27. These respectively state that every child has the right to the highest available standards of child care and the right to an adequate standard of living, although the report stresses that these are dependent on national definitions and the relevant society's commitment to resourcing. It also highlights the difficulty in making international comparisons about well-being since individual countries' data differs. A later UNICEF report (2013) measures well-being across five dimensions of material well-being, health and safety, education, behaviour and risks and housing and environment. These are broadly similar to those used in *America's Children: Key national indicators of well-being* (2011), although this explicitly includes family and social environments. The Australian Child Wellbeing Project, which focuses specifically on 8–14-year-olds, gathers children's perspectives and is based on the broader understanding of well-being as a child's material and environmental circumstances, relationships and how they see themselves in relation to those circumstances and relationships.

So there appears to be some broad agreement that well-being should extend beyond just a psychological perspective of good mental health to encompass all aspects of life but particularly engagement in and with society, which we might suppose requires us to have both a collective and an individual 'voice', so that what would seem to be central to any assessment of children's well-being are the views of children themselves – their subjective well-being. Diener (2000) puts forward three components of subjective well-being (SWB): children's own assessment, frequent positive emotions, infrequent negative ones and positive cognitive evaluation of either life as a whole or of specific domains such as school, family and community. SWB is the focus of research carried out by The Children's Society and the University of York to develop a robust, reliable and easily administered index to include domains, which young people, aged 8–16 have identified as important. Based on Heubner's Students' Life Satisfaction Scale (SLSS) developed in the US in the early 1990s and findings of their three previous reports of 2005, 2008 and 2010, they propose a five-point scale of qualitative statements scored from 1–5 to measure SWB and ten domains against which to measure specific well-being (Rees, Pople and Goswani 2011). But despite initiatives such as this, Butcher and Andrews (2009), in discussing the development of children's rights, highlight how little consultation with children there appears to be in policies designed for them. Further to this, Kellett (2011) remarks that prior to the 2007 launch in the UK of the Children's Plan, designed to meet the needs of both children and families, the consultation exercise involved professionals, parents and young people aged 16–19 but no direct consultation was sought with children below 16. Interestingly, although the Bailey report mentioned earlier canvassed the views of children and young people, the four headline themes only include specific reference to making parents' voices heard.

> The listening culture, so widely touted as essential to a better understanding of children's worlds and children's needs, appears to have completely bypassed a ten-year plan to deliver them a brighter future. (Kellet 2011, p.26)

The publication of the Children's Plan followed that of the 2007 UNICEF report, which found that the UK had the lowest level of overall well-being across the six recorded dimensions of material well-being, family and peer relationships, educational well-being, health and safety, behaviour and risks and subjective well-being (how young people rate their overall satisfaction with life). The United States (US) was just one place above, with Canada coming 12th and Denmark, Finland, Norway and Sweden all within the first third of the ranking. By 2013, based on the latest available data from 2009/2010, the UK's position had improved to 16th out of 29 countries (where previously there had only been 21) although this was measured against only five dimensions which again were different; family and peers and subjective well-being – the child's voice – having been dropped, but housing and environment included, thus making completely accurate comparison difficult. The US remained very low, coming 26th, Canada had fallen to 24th position, while Finland, Sweden and Norway remained in the first third, with Denmark just below. (Again there was no data for Australia and New Zealand.) The report noted that:

> As a moral imperative, the need to promote the well-being of children is widely accepted. As a pragmatic imperative, it is equally deserving of priority; failure to protect and promote the well-being of children is associated with increased risk across a wide range of later-life outcomes. (UNICEF Office of Research 2013, p.4)

While there may be broad agreement on what child well-being is, there are still some concerns about the resulting accuracy of any measure, but one would hope that all adults would recognise that how we treat our young people, or for that matter all groups within our communities, how we value them and the respect we accord them are indicators of the health of our society.

Political perspectives

There are those, however, who see a darker purpose behind the focus on reduced well-being.

Ecclestone and Hayes (2009) argue that it has left us all seeing ourselves as struggling to manage the negative emotional effects of life experiences, giving rise to a culture of the 'diminished self' in which we are all defined as having issues which can only be addressed by government-sponsored educational, social and welfare initiatives, or the plethora of available therapies. In short that we are told 'what to feel and what not to feel' (p.5), with education presenting a particular view of what it means to be human. They argue that:

> By…the depiction of 'complex needs' (as) caused by cycles of social and psychological deprivation…(and) claims that emotional dysfunction both arises from and contributes to inequality enable policy makers to focus on…emotional and social outcomes instead of material causes and effects (such as unemployment and the breakdown of communities). (p.12)

They note that the promotion of therapeutic orthodoxies such as 'we all suffer lasting legacies from the emotional effects of our childhood' (p.9) was particularly prevalent in the educational policies of the last Labour Government as evidenced by the renaming of the Department for Education and Skills (DfES) as the Department for Children, Schools and Families (DCSF) in 2007. This, they suggest, shifted the focus away from education based on intellectual disciplines and towards what they describe as therapeutic education; that is, a focus on the emotional needs and perceived emotional vulnerability of children. They attribute this to a rapidly developing victim culture arising from the death in 1997 of Diana, Princess of Wales, who they suggest was a 'model victim and martyr' (p.10).

In essence, it would appear that they are arguing against what might be perceived as state control of our emotional responses. And there may be some truth in this or at the very least some lessons to be learned about how, as previously discussed, a particular cultural view shapes policy which in turn feeds into our views, beliefs and attitudes about what is happening in our society. So perhaps, in order to avoid this cycle, we also need to look at measuring positive well-being, so we can be clear about how to improve things for our children. Yet, as a play therapist and specialist practitioner working with children with a range of presenting difficulties, I would argue that to write off all the evidence which points to the effects of our early experiences on later life would be counter-productive at best and irresponsible at worst. Interestingly, the Joseph Rowntree Foundation report *Poorer children: how important are attitudes and behaviour?* notes that evidence for the efficacy of:

> school- and local-based interventions designed to improve young people's social and emotional skills, behaviour and participation in positive activities is generally much weaker than our evidence on parent- and home-based interventions in the early years, and this evidence base needs to be strengthened. In particular, there is very little evidence on whether these (interventions) eventually lead to improved attainment at school. (Goodman and Gregg 2010, p.8)

Evidence for the efficacy of play and other creative arts therapies has been slow to accumulate, not least because therapists see research as impinging on the confidentiality of the therapy. Whether issues of confidentiality have more to do with the power relationship between client and therapist than 'ethical' practice is something that will be discussed in more detail later in this book. It would also be true to say that the evidence base for the effectiveness of creative arts therapy is growing as therapists become aware of the importance of undertaking research and providing robust pre- and post-intervention assessment data to inform case studies.

In parallel with the notion that policies for children do not include their views is the concern that government policies which are aimed at improving the lot of children and young people may also not come without an agenda. An example of this was

New Labour's pledge to combat child poverty and reduce social exclusion, which saw a strong link between child care policy and the 'welfare to work' reforms aimed at revitalising the labour market. While it may appear altruistic to encourage those on benefits, and particularly women, to move to employment and the prospect of an increased standard of living, the underlying driving force for this appears to have been an economic imperative to continue to feed the labour market (Norman 2009). There is complex interplay between the needs of those parents, often women, who want to stay at home to raise their children without this resulting in poor economic circumstances, the needs of those who want to balance family life with working but in jobs which pay at least a living wage and the desire of successive governments to boost tax revenue and decrease the so-called 'benefits bill'. Many of those jobs which women undertake are traditionally poorly paid, hence the need for cheaper and more accessible childcare. What this all suggests is a devaluing of the role of parent and carer by politicians who at the same time promote the idea of traditional family values, although exactly what these are is hard to determine since there is a wide range of differing family compositions within our society and much of the political discussion about families focuses on the move from benefits to work or whether same sex couples can really ever constitute a 'family' as it has been traditionally thought about.

There is a similar and equally complex relationship in education between the pressure resulting from the increase in testing and assessment in schools coupled with pressure to enter higher education, the resulting stress that young people say this creates as noted above and the need for the social and emotional welfare of our young people, which has been recognised as crucial to effective learning and development, to be catered for within the curriculum. Added to this are the pressures that many children and young people experience in relation to economic circumstances, which at the time of writing are impacting on more and more families as the real value of wages decreases and more families fall below the poverty line.

Although headlines in June 2013 from the Department of Work and Pensions say the number of children in workless poor families has reduced over the last year by 100,000, the overall number of children living in poverty (deemed as 60 per cent of median income) during 2011/2012 was 17 per cent or 2.3 million before housing costs had been included in calculations, and a staggering 27 per cent or 3.5 million after housing costs were taken into account. This is not say that only or all of those children living in poor households have low levels of well-being, for this would be to feed into the culture of demonisation of certain social groups favoured by the media and many politicians alike, but we need to be fully aware of the results of 'austerity measures' on real people and see them for what they are, a political ideology rather than the only economic solution. The impact of these policies of the Coalition Government was poignantly summed up by residents of Birmingham's Ladywood area as 'stress, depression, low self-esteem and lack of hope (which all) highlight the mental impact of austerity measures and media rhetoric about poverty' (O'Hara 2013).

Before becoming Prime Minister, David Cameron stated that 'the restoration of family values and a new commitment to economic and social responsibility are the key to repairing "broken Britain"' (Prince 2009). However, Jones (2011) suggests that it is this very 'doctrine of personal responsibility applied to a whole range of social problems affecting certain working class communities' which creates a culture of demonisation and results in those within these communities as being seen as only having themselves to blame (p.183).

Blaming and shaming whole communities of people for circumstances beyond their control seems not only unnecessarily harsh, but entirely counter-productive to achieving the kind of society that most of us would like to see where compassion and humanity are not seen as the province of the left-wing idealists or a 'fluffy' therapeutic community but as the indicator of an equal society that values all.

The fact that children growing up in poorer families in general achieve considerably lower levels of educational attainment is noted by Goodman and Gregg (2010) as a major contributing factor to patterns of social mobility and poverty. From analysis of four major longitudinal studies of children growing up some significant influences could be identified, including:

- *In early years:* the richness of the early home learning environment.

- *At primary school:* maternal aspirations for higher education, how far parents and children believe their own actions can affect their lives, and children's behavioural problems.

- *During secondary school:* teenagers' and parents' expectations for higher education, access to material resources, and engagement in anti-social behaviour.

- *Across childhood:* an important part of the story is about the transfer of cognitive abilities from one generation to the next.

To counteract poverty and boost social mobility needs real commitment from a government to look at the root causes in an objective way, rather than contribute to the problem with knee-jerk policies which in reality only compound the problem.

'Pink and blue moulds' – the growth of gender stereotyping

Beder *et al.* (2009) consider that there has been a rapid decline in well-being as a result of 'corporate' interference which has led to the transformation of play into a 'commercial opportunity' (p.3). This opportunity comes through the array of consumer durables owned by children: computers with internet access, televisions, mobile phones and more recently tablets, which have provided huge possibilities in terms of social networking, information access and a way of understanding their world but have also exposed them to what some see as the dangers of consumerism. Add to this this increased purchasing power of young people through both earnings from part-time jobs and 'pocket money' and you have a group which has attracted massive marketing attention (Layard and Dunn 2009).

Rather than technological advances per se being responsible for a shift in the context of childhood, it is then the way in which adults conceptualise childhood and project these ideas through available 'screens' which needs to be given fuller consideration in our construction of what is an appropriate childhood (Lee and Eke

2009). As has been noted, the prevailing culture in any society reflects a view of childhood which in turn shapes the way children view themselves. I have already referred to the way in which adverts for toys were heavily gender stereotyped when my children were growing up, and this continues to be the case. I recently visited Hamleys in London and was horrified by the overwhelmingly pink nature of the girls' department. 'Toys' focused on dolls, elaborate princess or fairy dressing-up outfits, make-up, jewellery and painted nails. A look at the website for Toys R Us, a major retailer, shows that boys' toys focus on action and girls' toys on caring activities or being beautiful, and even the Early Learning Centre, which appears to be much less gender specific, sells some toys in two colour versions so that a brush, wheelbarrow and cooking pans come in pink and another, less overtly 'feminine' colour such as blue, green or red. On the 'playing house' page, again both boys and girls feature with household items, although it is only girls who are depicted ironing and doing the washing, with many of the items associated with making tea, or teatime being predominantly pink. The more society promotes the idea that 'boys will be boys', generally meaning that they are noisy, active, determined and often difficult to control, the more parents are likely to see the more positive of these traits in a girl as unusual, tom-boyish or just plain wrong. Similarly, any boy who tends towards being like a 'girl', perceived as quiet, well behaved, gentle and nurturing, would be viewed as a bit of an oddity. Walter, writing in *Living Dolls* (2012) describe this stereotyping as 'pink and blue moulds' and suggests that:

> When girls and boys fall in with expectations, the stereotypes are reinforced and strengthened. Every aggressive boy feeds the stereotypes that are given to us by traditions and the new biological determinism; every aggressive girl is an unforgettable anomaly. (p.200)

I would argue, however, that rather than aggressive girls being seen just as an anomaly, they are often even more feared than aggressive boys simply because they are outside the pink mould and are therefore seen as completely unpredictable. Working in a secondary school some years ago, I was supporting a teenage girl whose response to anything new or any situation that changed unexpectedly was a loud verbal outpouring, often abusive, about how hopeless she felt we were, along with a high level of physical activity which led to her running around the outside the buildings, banging on the windows and, on one occasion, lying across the receptionist's desk for the best part of an hour, to stop a phone call home to her parents. It was this physical response which staff found most difficult to cope with and yet the same response from boys was expected and accepted as normal and they were therefore able to 'discipline' it. This girl's behaviour left everyone suggesting that there must be something significantly wrong with her, not because she couldn't handle change and uncertainty herself but because she 'acted like a boy'.

We are all individual and as a friend of Walter's noted when asked if she thought boys and girls were innately different '…boys and boys are different and so are girls and girls' (2010, p.199). As long as these stereotypes are promoted, the need for children to want to fit in with their peers and not feel excluded means they are often under pressure to conform to these almost caricatured roles. In adolescence, the need for acceptance becomes stronger for many young people, as does pressure from peers to conform to group expectations.

A place for therapy in education?

So increasing resilience would appear to be important if young people are to resist these pressures and maintain a positive view of themselves. This brings us back to promoting well-being through the school curriculum. If we set aside the idea explored earlier that the more we hand over to the Government of the day to take charge of, the more policies will determine and shape our actions, attitudes and beliefs, we might look instead at why school is a place where we can offer additional support to young people to increase well-being and develop resilience. Since school is a place that we can be fairly reliably assured nearly all young people will pass through, and good emotional health and well-being are cornerstones of being available to learn effectively, it would appear to follow that it is a good place for young people to access this support. My decision to train as a play therapist resulted from years of working with children who, to my thinking, had been failed by the school system and yet were only ever really offered more of the same when they were struggling to engage with learning and form relationships with staff and peers. Although Child and Adolescent Mental Health Services (CAMHS) would sometimes offer play therapy sessions, these were generally dependent on the parents' engagement with the service and also took place in a setting unfamiliar to the child. Offering therapeutic work within a place known to the child, which could be accessed with parental agreement but without their attendance, seemed to me at least to be offering the child a different opportunity to develop the more positive attachments, a stronger sense of self and a greater level of resilience needed to re-engage with learning and rebuild relationships. While I would recognise that the CAMHS approach may well have been born from the belief that although it is often the 'difficult' child who triggers a referral, it is the family that is in need of therapy, denying children the opportunity for change and development and better educational experiences seems to go against the idea of being child-centred, which good education should be. Some may argue that for our most disengaged young people, school is often the problem and so any solution associated with it or offered through it can be seen to be tainted and therefore undesirable. While this may be true in a small number of cases, my experience suggests that even when relationships have broken down significantly, there is usually one person whom the child sees as a trustworthy adult. If the therapist is not a member of the school staff, and can therefore be seen by the child as 'independent', then there is a basis for work which can be brokered between the three parties.

Reduced access to outdoor spaces

I have previously discussed that equally as important as considering whether government initiatives are as benign as they seem is the need to question how much of children's lives are regulated and determined by policies and services that purport to be child-centred but do not include children's views. An area where one might suggest it is not only apt but also crucial that young people's voices are heard is in the provision and construction of leisure and play spaces. Bailey and Barnes (2009) consider it imperative and suggest that a 'language and dialogue needs to be developed which does not patronize, is not tokenistic and which allows children to express their views and to have those valued throughout the design process' (p.190). And this is crucial at this time in our society since the move away from outdoor play and the associated estrangement from nature for our children reflect that shift away from the authoritative parent to one who may be seen as out of touch with children's needs because they focus more on what they perceive the children want (Frost 2010).

At a recent function I was seated opposite two girls aged around ten years old. Making conversation, I asked them what they liked to do when they weren't at school. 'Well', said one, 'I do violin on Mondays, on Tuesday it's dance class, Wednesday is drama group and on Thursday it's French club after school. Oh yes, and Fridays I go swimming!' 'Good heavens', I replied, 'you are busy! Do you ever just loaf around and do nothing?' 'Oh no!' she responded, 'I don't do anything like that!' To me this seems to epitomise the over-directed and busy lives many of our children are subject to, where every moment is gainfully employed and thinking and being time is carefully scheduled in as 'down' time, 'me' time or 'leisure activities'. I recall a Schulz 'Peanuts' cartoon of many years ago where Charlie Brown, Linus and Lucy were all lying on a hilltop, watching the clouds and describing what they saw...a dragon...a sailing ship...a castle...a horse or whatever else their imagination could conjure up. It is this that prevailing attitudes seem to have diminished – this undirected, unstructured free and 'being' time where children just are! So much of what they do seems to be constructed and over-managed, which may in part reflect the earlier admission age for schooling and a rapid expansion of pre-school, nursery and after-school provision which has led to increased institutionalisation of playing time for children; yet another province of adult organisation and direction (Tovey 2007). This, combined with a generalised fear for their safety, results in more and more children being transported to and from pre-school, primary school and other activities, which in turn means more vehicles on the road. This then creates a vicious circle where adult concerns for safety lead to action which creates more concerns for safety in a time when children are said to be statistically safer than ever before. However, Gill (2007) urges caution for the idea that children are less at risk as pedestrians and discusses how evidence suggests this is because fewer and fewer children are out and about on our streets. Where once they played outside their houses, on derelict land and down alleyways, now they are safe indoors with screen-based games and the television, away from the potential harm of the traffic, strangers and uneven, slippery surfaces.

Gill discusses how changes in childhood's domain are in part a symptom of risk aversion, but are mainly a side-effect of wider social, cultural and economic changes. The growth of road traffic and car-dependent lifestyles, parents' longer working hours, a decline in quantity and quality of public space and the growth of indoor leisure activities have all reinforced the logic of containment (p.14). Adults' perception of the risk children are at certainly plays a part in the decline in play in the streets and other public places and the increased access to home-based activities or play which take place in commercial settings, but there are other factors. The growth of indoor leisure activities reflects the significant change in the nature of spaces where children can and do play. As housing has expanded, so have the infrastructures needed to support them, reducing access to open fields and increasing traffic as adults travel further afield to work, and expensive and poorly integrated public transport leads to increased reliance on cars.

Although many estates have play areas, they are often limited in size, activities are prescribed and even the noise from playing children is unwelcome by many. This change in children's experience of leisure activities needs to be set against the wider context of change for the whole of society as a result of a greater focus on entertainment within the home, partly as a result of almost universal television ownership and increased ownership of entertainment centres, computers and mobile phones. These all provide access to both the commercial and social world and it has become increasingly difficult to be part of these without engaging with the mass media which feeds general interest in the news, opinion, reality TV and the lives of celebrities. There is also within society, a sense that access to much of our rural landscapes is restricted as a result of intensification of agriculture and a cultural fear of trespass, despite the access rights granted as a result of lengthy struggles by the working classes.

Use of commercial play spaces has increased as access to our open spaces has decreased. Many of these are branded, located in shopping areas or attached to pubs and restaurants and are much more prevalent in urban areas. This in itself raises two important issues; first there is the cost and second, transportation. With cuts to public transport in many rural areas and the increased and often prohibitive cost of that which does exist, travelling to many of these commercial activities is pricey, as is the entrance fee, and this puts them out of the reach of many families on lower incomes. But rather than just replacing outdoor environments, Bailey and Barnes (2009) suggest that this type of activity may be more about parents feeling they are addressing the needs of their children, easing their own consciences for limiting play time and also gaining some quality time for themselves.

One of the major issues that commercial play spaces raise is how much they are about what children would want as play spaces, how much they are about adult perceptions of what they would find inviting and exciting and how much about manageability or control. Are they just another example of adults defining the concept of childhood without including children's views? For healthy development in childhood, it is important to be able to explore freely, to create our own 'small' environments, to take risks and to challenge ourselves. Play, in being creative and satisfying, is often messy and noisy and certainly uncontained and these three elements can be very unwelcomed by adults so that play appears to be something that intrudes into well-ordered and efficient adult lives; play has become an inconvenience.

A survey of 3,000 parents, children and adults conducted by Play England, Play Wales, Play Scotland and PlayBoard Northern Ireland and published on 7 August 2013 to mark Playday, the national day of play, indicates that in addition to traffic and stranger danger, what stops parents letting their children outside to play is intolerant neighbours and fear of being judged by them if their children are out playing unsupervised. Parents are also concerned that ball games and noise will cause problems if none already exist. Bailey and Barnes (2009) cite the case in 2005 of the Jigsaw Nursery in Hampshire which was 'advised by Fareham Borough Council to restrict children to only one hour's outside play following complaints from neighbours about noise' (p.17), and Gill (2007) reports that three 12-year-olds were arrested and DNA tested by the police in Halesowen in 2006. Their 'crime' had been climbing a tree on public land. West Midlands Police saw this act of anti-social behaviour as needing to be dealt with robustly to prevent more serious incidents from developing. Gill goes onto recognise that although incidents such as those cited above may be rare, they do represent evidence of over-reaction to children's activities and a growing trend for imposition of formal sanctions by the police and other public bodies.

Under the Environmental Protection Act of 1990, although children playing is not a statutory noise nuisance, councils do have the statutory duty to investigate all noise complaints. In 2011, this led to *The Telegraph* headline, 'Couple threatened with fine over noisy four-year-old son'. Because the council was compelled to investigate, the couple had received a letter outlining the possible proceedings, including a £5,000 fine, with an additional £500 per day if the noise continued after a noise-abatement notice had been issued. Action to determine whether the noise seriously affected the near neighbour's peace and quiet of the home could have included monitoring equipment or a visit to the complainant by an environmental health officer to gain first-hand experience of the noise level. It appeared highly unlikely that a noise-abatement notice would be the outcome but as the father of the four-year-old boy in question noted, 'My son can be noisy and boisterous, but he is just a normal four year old playing in the garden. It's the summer holidays, for goodness sake. Children need to play outside. What am I supposed to do, gag him and put him in his bedroom?' (*The Telegraph* 2011).

The nature of play

And he is of course right, children need to play, inside and outside, since play is at the heart of our children's holistic development. But what is play? Frost (2010) suggests that although scholars throughout the 20th century have tried to define play, as of yet there is no clear or unequivocal definition. He notes that, historically, children's play has been set in a variety of 'playgrounds' – wilderness, fields, streams, gardens, farmland, the seashore, parks and vacant ground – and that it has been both free and spontaneous. The National Playing Fields Association, in its 2000 document *Best Play: what play provision should do for children*, suggests, 'Play is freely chosen, personally directed, intrinsically motivated behaviour that actively engages the child' (p.6).

Play Wales extends this, suggesting that children and young people determine and control the content and intent of their play by following their own instincts, ideas and interests, in their own way, for their own reasons, while the Welsh Assembly Government notes that children use play in the natural environment to learn of the world they inhabit with others. It is the very process of learning and growth, and as such all that is learned through it, that is of benefit to the child. This is underlined by evidence from research by Taylor, Kuo and Sullivan (2001) into the connection between attention deficit disorder and 'green' play spaces. Their study examined the relationship between children's nature exposure through leisure activities and their attentional functioning and found that children functioned better than usual after activities in green settings defined as mostly natural areas such as parks, farmyards or the green backyard of neighbourhood spaces.

Bruce (2001), in discussing learning through play, reminds us that 'play is influenced by culture, setting and atmosphere, and that it is the highest form of learning' (p.v). Tovey (2007) considers the fluid and evolving qualities of play, suggesting that rather than play fitting neatly into pre-defined categories such as imaginative, problem solving or exploratory, it shifts between them, flowing from one to another and back again, particularly in the outdoors, where features of the environment add to the momentum. But above all, play should be free from adult interference and from their misconceptions of the risks it poses. That is not to say that we should intentionally endanger children nor that adults have no place in their play but that the adults' role should be defined by the child so that play remains child-led and adult supported. This is emphasised in the approach of the Danish Nature School, in Globussen. Children attend Globussen from the ages of three to seven and in outdoors activities on the beach, the children are accompanied by their kindergarten teachers but are encouraged to be as independent as possible, dressing themselves, collecting tools and exploring freely. Parents are involved in an experiential way as they build the storage structures that are used, creating a family and community dimension which provides a safe and functional base for the children to enhance their independence, not limit it.

Louv (2005) describes how natural play has become 'criminalised' illustrating this with the story of American John Rick, his family and the Scripps Ranch Community Association. The Rick family moved to Scripps Ranch because of its child-friendly reputation and vast areas of open, natural play space. Several years after moving, the activities of the children – making tree houses, damming up streams, making bike jumps – were being described as 'illegal' uses of the land by the Community Association. Regulations about where children could play were tightened and parents provided activities such as basketball hoops in their yards and gardens. The children moved their biking activities to the ends of drives and the Community Association told parents they were violating the covenants they had signed. As a result, the children moved indoors, grew unfit and overweight and parents ended up transporting them ten miles to a neighbouring skatepark.

It is interesting therefore to note that further findings from the Play England et al. report reveal that around 40–45 per cent of parents feel that children playing outside can help to unite communities and help families get to know each other, and a third of adults surveyed and a fifth of children wanted more spaces to play out in within their local community. Sixty per cent of parents said they would feel confident to let their children out if others were also playing outside.

Bailey and Barnes (2009) describe how socio-economic and cultural differences impact on the spaces and places available for children's play, highlighting Office for National Statistics figures which put the number of children under the age of two who live in homes two or more storeys above ground as around 58,000, noting that these children would be unable to access outdoor play spaces without being accompanied. Adults surveyed by The Children's

Society (2008) were asked at what age they felt children should go out unsupervised and, not surprisingly, only three per cent said under the age of eight, while 79 per cent said over the age of 11 with 43 per cent of those feeling that 14 and over was the right age. These kind of statistics make the provision of safe, local play areas even more imperative, but not spaces which are so safe as to inhibit challenge and risk taking, rather spaces which have been developed as a result of consultation with the users themselves. Gill (2007) argues that while risk is easily calculated and evidenced through accident and injury statistics, the benefits of risk and challenge for children's development have a much less secure evidence base, although many would disagree, as will be discussed in Chapter 3. To counteract this, he suggests that what is needed is for society to 'embrace a philosophy of resilience' (p.82), in order to change the focus from 'adults' duty of care to children's agency' (p.84).

Effects on health

Another result of the decrease in outdoor play is a lack of fitness and increasing numbers of overweight and obese children, again a topic that has been consistently hailed by the media as a blight of our time. Advertising for so called 'junk' foods is estimated at hundreds of millions of pounds in the UK, while the Health Survey for England of 2011 notes that in 2010, over 30 per cent of 2–15-year-olds were either overweight or obese, with rates being higher in urban areas and for those whose parents were either overweight or obese. Government projections based on current trends suggest that in 20 years, around 75 per cent of adults will suffer from obesity-related illnesses such as diabetes and heart disease and many more will be at risk of liver disease as a result of the binge-drinking culture of recent years, so this is a serious cause for concern. However, under the current drive for 'austerity' wages have decreased in real terms and many more families are living below the poverty line. With the cost of feeding a family increasing all the time with rising food and energy prices, many more people's diets are likely to contain the kind of food that can lead to increased weight and unhealthy lifestyles. When people are 'living on the edge' the focus of their energies is survival which may not leave much time or inclination to source healthier food options (Health and Social Care Information Centre 2012).

The plethora of fast food outlets and an increase in ready meals or food that requires little preparation have become strong features of our social culture and while there may be scant proof of the negative effect of commercialisation on children, there is evidence from OFCOM's 2004 report into food advertising that it 'had a modest direct effect on children's food choices and a larger but unquantifiable indirect effect on children's food preferences, consumption and behaviour'. As a result, there are strict 'rules' about both the content and scheduling of advertisements centred around foods that are high in fat, salt and sugar (HFSS). The code states that food and drink adverts must not condone or encourage poor nutritional habits and unhealthy lifestyles, use hard-sell techniques or use licensed characters or celebrities who are popular with children, the latter only applying if adverts are specifically targeted at pre-school and primary age children. The code also states that adverts for HFSS foods cannot appear around programmes commissioned for or likely to appeal to children under the age of 16, and there are to be none at all on dedicated children's channels. Alongside these rules there is the constant push from the Government for us all to lead a healthier lifestyle, such as the NHS Change for Life campaign and the prospect of increased participation in sport and leisure activities as a result of the Olympic legacy. However, despite the hopes, research from University College London's Institute of Child Health following the Olympics found that 38 per cent of girls and 63 per cent of boys, around half of all seven-year-olds, were exercising for less than the recommended one hour a day. Rather than showing increased participation, the study showed that it had fallen to the lowest level for five years, with around 25 per cent of girls having done no sport at all in the month preceding the survey. This can surely not have been helped by the Coalition Government's programme of selling off school playing fields and the scrapping of legal quotas for team sports. The lack of physical activity also reflects the loss of curriculum time for sports activities and a reduction in break time that has occurred in many schools, particularly at lunch time, often in an effort to reduce the supposed opportunities for misbehaviour. So yet again we are giving our children mixed messages, since reduction in recreation time and facilities in schools is at odds with the healthier lifestyle message promoted by a ban on sweets, crisps and fizzy drinks in schools and celebrity chefs such as Jamie Oliver championing the cause of healthier school meals. These are underpinned by government standards which include strict guidance on how many times a week unhealthy burgers and sausages can be served and the number of portions of fruit and vegetables that must be available to children each day in order that they have a healthy balanced diet. Interestingly, while such guidance applies to all local authority controlled schools, academies are merely encouraged to adopt the standards, something which Oliver sees as 'illogical, unreasonable and weird' (Low and Barnes 2012). It could be argued that by focusing on food and healthy eating, rather than access to outdoor facilities, the Government is attempting to put responsibility back into the growing lap of the consumer rather than considering the underlying causes which just might have more to do with government policies, austerity measures and increasing poverty than our own unhealthy values. More recently, Oliver himself was heavily criticised for comments he made about those who are poor eating chips and cheese in front of a massive television, suggesting their priorities were skewed and that they might choose healthier foodstuffs over home entertainment. This is further evidence of the temptation to demonise low income groups within society, as further underlined by a suggestion from Eastlands Homes, a not-for-profit housing association in Manchester for those facing cuts to benefits as a result of the so-called 'bedroom tax', 'Can you really afford Sky, cigarettes, bingo, drinks and other non essentials? If your benefit is being cut and you want to keep your home you have to make up the difference. Non-essential items won't matter if you lose your home. Start budgeting now – we can help you do this, call us!' (Latent Existence 2013).

It might be argued that unless we have experienced restricted income ourselves, we are in no position to pass judgement on what money might be spent on. If money for over-priced commercial entertainment such as cinema complexes, theatres, sports events, concerts and eating out is severely limited, then being able to smoke, have a drink or two and watch the television might just make the difference between sustaining some sense of well-being and falling into a deep depression.

Paradoxically, much of this discourse on childhood has been about adults: their perceptions of what it is like to be a child, their fears for young people's safety and well-being, the way they have developed our landscapes, the policies they make and how the media shapes their attitudes and in turn those of their children. I would suggest that this highlights the significant imbalance of power between children and adults that exists in a culture where news coverage of young people can at best be neutral and worst negative.

Gill's idea of a philosophy of resilience and agency parallels that of play therapy. In drawing this comparison, I do not suggest that play therapy is a panacea for all the ills of our children and it is important to keep a real perspective about the number of young people who have such low levels of well-being that their life chances are significantly affected. The Good Childhood report of 2012 notes that:

> Many children in the UK are happy with their lives. However, substantial numbers of children do not feel so positive. At any given time, around 4 per cent of eight-year-olds and 14 per cent of 15-year-olds have low 'subjective well-being'...or happiness with their lives as a whole. In total it can be estimated that around half a million children in the UK in the eight to 15 age range have low well-being at any point in time. (p.5)

For these young people, their level of unhappiness is more than just dissatisfaction with some aspects of life so that they rarely feel safe at home within their family, among their friends or at school. The long-term impacts can leave them open to bullying and victimisation, see them behaving in ways which are risky to both themselves and others, reduce their educational opportunities and lead to anxiety related disorders and depression (The Children's Society 2012).

However, what these young people need is not sympathy, or even empathy – they need us to be pro-active in the manner of authoritative parents, to take charge and support them in a way that allows them to develop a positive sense of self that encourages resilience building and helps them to become independent and autonomous. We should not see them as victims or demonise them but develop positive relationships with them that recognise they are open to exploitation by commercial organisations, can feel pressured by an overtly sexualised society, have become disconnected from nature but have their own culture which we should respect, and have the capacity to be discerning and informed participants in society. For those who have had difficult life experiences, we may need to offer them therapeutic opportunities which recognise that often words are hard to find –this can be the place of play therapy. If we then take that play therapy outdoors we are offering them a very real, dynamic and creative environment which will enhance the therapeutic process and reconnect them to the land on which they live.

Chapter 3

The Importance of the 'Body' Self

This chapter will consider aspects of child development highlighting the importance of the physical 'body' self in relation to attachment theory. It will focus on the embodiment, projection and role (EPR) paradigm put forward by Jennings which informs non-directive play therapy practice. It will discuss the importance of resilience building and risk taking in healthy social and emotional development and how play therapy contributes to this It will draw together previous chapters to provide the rationale for using the outdoors in therapy with children to create a lifelong attachment to the 'nature mother'.

> The baby's earliest form of play is in the extension of the normal handling he receives from his mother in the daily routine of feeding, bathing and nursing. Mother rocks the baby, hugs him, plays with his toes and lets him grasp her finger. These forms of physical contact help the baby to define the limits of his own body. (Chown 1963, p.21)

The body self

The first client I worked with was a boy of five who was attending a nurture group set within his mainstream primary school. His mother was suffering from depression and his home life was often somewhat chaotic, with older siblings who were overtly physical in their relationship with him. He had no experience of being held gently and safely by an attuned adult. Within his nurture group, he was often physically 'uncontained', running around, shouting loudly, rolling on the floor and frequently running off around the school and grounds. As adults often then physically restrained him, he was getting the containment he needed but in a negative way that was impacting on his sense of well-being and putting him at risk of exclusion.

Within our sessions together in the ideal small, safe and contained playroom, he became more expansive in his use of paint, which he splashed everywhere, and the big sand tray which I used on the floor in an effort to ground him. He poured in all the available water, took off his shoes and socks and splashed and jumped and stamped with all his energy. Then he suddenly took off his shirt, went to take off his shorts and pants and shouted, 'Me lie down!' He wanted to immerse himself totally in the wet sand, and I could sense his desire and need for some 'womblike' containment and concrete, sensory feedback in order to begin to understand his body and how it felt to be physically connected and contained. I explained that his clothes were not for taking off although his shoes and socks were but I felt that in doing this, he had been denied what he really needed and that this was not the child-centred practice I wanted to engage in. On the one hand, the small, safe playroom was needed to give him a concept of physical containment, but on the other hand, he needed 'big' expansive sensory experiences where he felt things directly on his skin at a conscious and concrete level in order to be able to accept that physical containment.

In discussion with my supervisor, we agreed that the use of some of the activities outlined by Sherbourne (2001) for developing body awareness were necessary. Sherbourne suggests that babies' bodies melt and mould themselves into the body of the containing adults who hold and carry them. It is this holding that gives the feeling of safety and containment and that is crucial to our ability to 'respond to human contact and form relationships' (p.38). She describes her approach as relationship play and suggests three types of relationship: caring or 'with', 'shared' (as with a mother and baby), and 'against' (where we test our strength against the bodies of others, p.39). However, I was mindful of the fact that many of the 'with' activities she presents involve close body contact, which works well with more than one child but is not generally advisable when the therapist and child are alone. (The importance of touch is discussed later in this chapter and again in Chapter 4.)

My supervisor and I agreed that additional parental consent would be best for physical 'body' work but also that I would steer clear of the 'with' activities, showing these to the school staff instead so that they could be done with a peer within the nurture group. I then work on 'shared' and 'against' activities for a short time at the start of play therapy sessions. Over time, he developed a much stronger sense of his physical self and his need to run around, roll on the floor and shout loudly in order to gain some sensory feedback was significantly diminished. However, I can't help but think that had we been able to access an outdoor space where he could have experienced the wind, rain and sun on his skin, been wrapped tightly in warm clothing or felt the breeze through his t-shirt and hair, jumped in puddles and stamped in mud, rolled down slopes, crawled through small spaces and taken some physical risk within the safety of the therapeutic relationship, it would have provided a much more real physical experience and more meaningful engagement with the world as explored through the case studies in Part II of this book.

In the first chapter I discussed how, in recent times, a variety of organisations have utilised outdoor experiences as a way for people to understand the idea of the multi-faceted relationships that we have with ourselves, with others and with our natural environments. What comes through most strongly in their varied approaches is a desire to support the development of young people's autonomy – their ability to take charge of and understand themselves, to have self-awareness, and to understand that they can take action on their own behalf. Implicit in this are two key themes: the ability to challenge oneself and take risks, and a democratic approach to decision making. Both of these help to build resilience, that capacity we have to withstand what life throws at us, and which resonates with the core conditions of non-directive therapy, which will be discussed further in Chapter 4.

Popular theory would suggest that healthy development is dependent on a particular set of experiences but as Music notes (2011, p.7) 'exactly what is necessary for someone to become human is controversial…and can be based on cultural beliefs and prejudice'. This is borne out by the discussion in Chapter 2 where it was noted that adult perceptions of children's experiences of growing up may be considerably wide of the mark and heavily dependent on cultural misrepresentations of childhood as shown in the media. So any discussion of what constitutes good early experiences needs approaching with caution and a mind for cultural differences, although there is little doubt that in order to develop a sense of self, we need to be held in mind by and reflected through the eyes of others.

It is the development of this self-awareness which must be our starting point for without this how can we be aware of or know others? Without a relationship with our 'self', how can we know how to relate to those around us? Axline (1964), writing in *Dibs: In Search of Self* reflects that:

> When horizons grow or diminish within a person the distances are not measurable by other people. Understanding grows from personal experience that enables a person to see and feel in ways so varied and so full of changeable meaning that one's self-awareness is the determining factor. (p.15)

And yet, we need others to inform this, initially through the sensory feedback we get, starting in the womb. Jennings (2011) notes that our early attachment experiences are strongly influenced by our 'body' experiences and suggests these are encompassed within two paradigms: neuro-dramatic play (NDP), from conception to the time of collaboration at around six months, and embodiment, projection and role (EPR) from 'birth playing' to 'drama for real' at around seven years. She describes this stage of our development as Theatre of Body, a 'theatre in the round' between the mother and the baby, which is established through three primary circles of containment, care and attachment involving sensory, rhythmic and dramatic playfulness between the mother and unborn or newborn baby. Trevarthan (2004) puts forward a theory of companionship, both intimate and casually sociable, based on our deep-seated needs to make contact with one another through an innate musicality which uses rhythm and movement. So we cannot exist as a body alone, but we form relationships through and with our body or as our body. To engage in this relationship requires us to come into conscious being, what Damasio likens to stepping into the light, the moment when 'our sense of self moves into the world of the mental' (2000, p.3). Consciousness, he tells us, is the act of telling a story without words, the story of 'the how' our encounters with other objects or events within our immediate environment change our body states with the story told non-verbally, using a vocabulary of body signals. This he describes as a feeling of the feeling and the way in which we know life. But he also urges caution, noting that mind and consciousness are not the same thing and stating, 'There is more to mind than consciousness and there can be mind without consciousness' (p.27) as seen in patients who have one but not the other.

Gerhardt (2004, p.18) tells us that each of us is born with the ability to change and adapt to our circumstances, both internally and externally, via a complex system of chemical and electrical signals which arise out of a 'pulsating symphony of different body rhythms and functions', literally the rhythms of our life. It is through these systems that we try to establish our normal range of arousal and again we need the presence of others. The attentive mother figure soothes, calms and regulates our changing affect system to bring us back to homeostasis; we experience the calm after the storm. Without this re-regulating influence, we remain in a hyper-aroused state, our body rhythms and physiological systems disrupted to the extent that the development of the brain is affected.

> Children exposed to significant threat will 're-set' their baseline state of arousal such that even when no external threats or demands are present, they will be in a physiological state of persistent alarm...(they) will have an altered baseline such that an internal state of calm is rarely obtained. (Perry 2002)

Establishing playfulness

A key element of healthy early experiences is playfulness, both our own and that of the others we interact with. Playfulness arises out of the non-verbal 'dialogue' between the infant and their primary carer (mother figure) and is characterised by the to and fro of action and reaction, creating interaction, the precursor to more complex social communication and language development.

Initially this may be seen as movement with which the infant attempts to communicate an interest, an internal impulse to seek conscious awareness displayed by movement and voice exploring exchanges in the external reality. The movement also implies intent, a connection to the future which Trevarthen (2004) suggests demonstrates a self that is not just receiving comfort, but actively seeking out the self of the other. From the earliest moments after birth the baby is seeking interaction, mirroring the expressions it sees in the faces around it. Although some may suggest this is not meaningful interaction, recent discoveries in neuroscience have shown the existence of mirror neurons which evidence this capacity to understand what others are experiencing from within ourselves; to make a connection and to do so from these earliest moments after birth. Zeedyk and Robertson's documentary film *The Connected Baby* highlights how these early responses, long thought to have no real meaning, do in fact mean something to the mother; that this is the way of the baby saying, 'I'm here, I'm with you, I'm connected'. So in seeking this connection through interaction, we develop embodied meaning; the body and mind together, not as separate entities, nor merely working together in tandem but 'a body mind wholism – a unity of which "body" and "mind" are each partial facets' (Totton 2003, p.29).

Playfulness is not dependent on visible and audible responses, it can also occur during pregnancy. Many mothers will have conversations with the unborn baby, rhythmically stroke their belly or play music to them. Parents may give the baby a nick-name even before they know the gender, evidence of the desire to 'personalise' it, to make it a real part of their relationship, to establish a connection with it. These actions are all part of the development of playfulness. Where there is playfulness, there is generally also attunement, affection and affirmation, the cornerstones of healthy attachment which create the map for our future relationships and ways of being. It is usually these positive and fulfilling early experiences which have been missing or damaged for many children who come to play therapy.

For those children whose early experiences have been characterised by inconsistent or tentative handling, physical or sexual abuse, injury or illness the sense of the body self can be seriously impaired or missing altogether. The type of touch received in the first months structures our subjective relationship with our body which, when positive, gives us feelings of being alive, of vitality and of living in our body self (Orbach 2003), and of having a robust physicality, a core physical resilience with which to build our connections to others, to begin to be playful and so to begin to learn. Without this, as Orbach goes on to tell us, our body is merely a 'surface; body as symbol, body not as lived experience but body as text on which we inscribe the desperateness of not having an alive body but only a facsimile body' (p.40). Without our sense of body self, we inhabit a cold, flat, dull and two-dimensional body rather than one which is warm, pulsating, rhythmic and alive to the experiences created by, with and through the 'others' in our lives. In later years, we will be left still struggling to make a real connection to our body and in trying to establish one may resort to gaining feedback in unhealthy ways such as through disordered eating, through substance abuse or acts of self-harm.

If you watch newborn babies when they are alone, they do not lie still and silent, cut off from their environment. They move and are vocal beyond their cries of hunger or discomfort. They stretch their limbs, they kick and move their hands and arms, they gurgle and 'mew'. They are developing their body awareness, learning about its capacity for movement and about the space it occupies. These experiences are fed by the infants' senses and are the beginnings of what Piaget termed 'sensorimotor play' which is further developed by the interaction with the mother figure. Playfulness develops within the space between the mother figure and the infant, the space which Winnicott describes as the 'intermediate' playground (1971, p.47). Jennings (2011) stresses how important touch and the actions of holding, feeding, massaging, stroking and bathing are to the development of the body self without which, playfulness will not develop. These meetings of the two, the mother figure and the baby, often give rise to routines which are anticipated by both and established through the act of caring, of meeting the infants' needs. Initially, the mother figure responds to the baby's attempts at connection in a playful way, mirroring their actions, but gradually she begins to initiate some of the play and activities become co-constructed in meaning; they have an intimacy which comes from shared understanding and the sense of connection. Cattanach (1999), writing about co-construction in play therapy, tells us that 'our knowledge of the world is constructed between people. Shared versions of knowledge are constructed in the course of everyday lives together' (p.80). And so it is with the mother figure and infant. The everyday activities of feeding, changing, soothing and playing keep the connection real and immediate.

The play between the two takes on a rhythm of its own – they establish their own routines and rituals which give rise to turn taking and negotiation, important in the development of language and communication. When my own children were babies, we played a game of 'babyrobics' at changing time, involving our gently exercising their arms and legs in a rhythmic action which mirrored the activities of aerobic exercise. 'Windmilling' arms and attempts to get their legs mimicking the action of a fast runner always produced gurgles, giggles and small squeals of delight! While there will be cultural differences in the rituals and routines that are established throughout our lives they will remain an important feature of our sense of well-being, providing predictability, security and structure and marking both important occasions and experiences and the passing of time.

Developing secure attachments

Much has been written about attachment and the following sources will provide you with a broader, more detailed understanding of the concept: Bowlby (1988), Hughes (1996), Howe et al. (1999), Goldberg (2000) and Gerhardt (2004).

Attachment describes the dependency relationship between the developing infant and the primary caregiver (who I have termed the 'mother figure') and develops through three stages: pre-attachment, attachment in the making and clear cut attachment as described by Ainsworth (Goldberg 2000), giving us what has become known as a 'secure base' (Bowlby 1988). Clear cut attachment or the formation of a special relationship depends on the infant understanding that 'an enduring specific other exists apart from concrete interactive experiences' and develops during the second half of the first year (Goldberg 2000, p.17). Although the focus was originally on the mother and infant relationship, it is now recognised that the primary attachment figure, while frequently the mother, may also be a significant 'other', such as the father, grandparent, foster parent or nanny. The key element of the attachment relationship is that physical care and emotional containment are consistently attended to through the mother figure's attunement to the infant's needs and affirmation of and affection towards their developing spirit, their uniqueness. In essence, 'the baby needs a caregiver who identifies with them so strongly that the baby's needs feel like hers; (the infant) is physiologically and psychologically an extension of her' (Gerhardt 2004, p.23).

Being the central focus of a carer who adapts readily to the infant's needs instils in the baby a sense of 'omnipotency', of having power and of being loveable. As their relationship develops and the infant begins to understand that they are physically separate from the mother figure and that each has their own emotional experiences, the infant gives back some of the power to the parent so that their relationship and interactions become co-constructed, allowing for healthy individuation; the recognition of the self as a separate entity from the mother figure and our early steps towards independence and autonomous actions.

From attachment to the mother figure the infant is able to make new relationships so that there are multiple attachment figures as their world expands to include more shared parenting, the wider family and other caring adults such as friends or nursery staff. Pearce (2009) suggests that there is now considerable supporting evidence that children's social and emotional development is best predicted by a network of attachment figures rather than through the single relationship with the mother figure. So we move from the 'closed' circles of care, containment and attachment to an 'open' circle of trusting relationships which can only grow from that safety and security provided by our early relationship with our mother figure that allows us to trust and have hope for similar future relationships (Erikson 1965).

Developing schemas

Play develops from the sensory, physical activity of the body to incorporate objects through our developing ability to reach, to grasp and to put things into the mouth for further exploration. As the infant experiences more of the world, they develop an internal representation of these through what Piaget termed 'assimilation and accommodation'. In the process of taking in or assimilating the environment to its own activity, the infant incorporates experience into existing mental frameworks or schemas or what Bowlby referred to as our internal working model. When these experiences do not 'fit' easily with existing schemas this leads to accommodation, where the infant adjusts themself and the activity to the environment so refining the schema to accommodate this new experience. Athey (2007, p.95) describes schemas as 'patterns of repeatable actions that lead to early categories and then to logical classification'. This repetition of action is another facet of the rhythmical nature of our development. Stern conceptualised the process of the accumulation of the meanings of differing experiences, sensations, emotions, actions or perceptions as representations of interactions that have generalised (RIGs). In discussing Stern's work, (Santostefano 2004) notes that RIGs are compared with the individual components of the previous experience in a process Stern termed 'the evoked companion'. These enable the infant to determine whether the interaction being experienced differs from expectation based on previous experiences or if a significant change has taken place. If there are differences, which are sustained through further episodes of the action, then a new RIG is constructed representing the current experience. However, if the two representations are markedly different, the infant may experience some conflict.

The more consistent the responses from the 'mother figure', the less the conflict within and the more secure the sense of self. Santostefano further notes that evoked companions are also operating when the infant is playing alone so that in the play of the boy with the rocks detailed in the introductory chapter of this book, his feelings of pleasure and success would have stemmed from having previous successes greeted with enthusiasm and pleasure by significant others in his life. The consistent, attuned and predictable responses from the mother figure which give us our secure base build our resilience and empower us to take risks, engage with challenges and cope with difficult experiences and failures. They also give us our patterns for relating to others, constructively or destructively – patterns which may last throughout our lifespan unless we are given opportunities to experience those positive early attachments in a new, therapeutic relationship, such as a new relationship with a significant other or that offered by therapeutic interventions.

Cath Arnold (2010) and her team at the Penn Green Centre for Children and Families in Corby, Northamptonshire, have done much research into children's schemas and presenting issues of loss, attachment and separation which evidences possible links between schematic actions and the emotions they are experiencing. They have identified a number of 'observable patterns of repeated action', including connecting and disconnecting, proximity and separation, enclosure, enveloping, containing and transformation, which although not a repeated pattern, has been observed as the process that occurs as a result of some action such as sand becoming wet, resulting in a change of state. Transformation is a vital aspect of the play therapy process, giving children the opportunity to rework previous experiences and to transform the ending to find resolution. Arnold and her colleagues have also identified patterns of transporting, of carrying objects or of being carried from one place to another and suggest this may be representational of Winnicott's transitional object (pp.22–23). Arnold notes how a significant aspect of their study was the way children used schemas at a symbolic level and cites Piaget's ideas of conscious and unconscious symbolism with the deeper meanings being unconsciously expressed through projection of inner feelings onto familiar toys as a defence mechanism that protects them from direct experience of strong emotions such as anxiety and fear. Again, this parallels the processes in play therapy and underlines the power of symbolic distance, which allows for safe processing of difficult or traumatic experiences. As McCarthy tells us, 'We can't conquer death and the many terrifying aspects of living, but play and the symbols it produces can make this life not only bearable, but also a rich palette from which to express ourselves' (2012, p.50).

Affect attunement

As well as meeting the infant's physical or care needs, the mother supports the development of emotional regulation through the process of affect attunement. During the early experiences in the first few months after birth, the mother identifies so strongly with the infant that its needs feel like her needs so if it feels bad, she will feel bad and will want to make the infant feel comfortable again. She initially responds to the infant non-verbally through actions such as stroking, soothing, rocking, feeding and through her tone of voice and facial expressions. In order to soothe the fractious and distressed infant, she enters its emotional state, and through initially mirroring its loud cries with her tone, she leads the infant to a calmer state by regulating her tone, by bringing it down until the infant is re-regulated to a happy and comfortable state which she herself will also then experience (Gerhardt 2004).

Parents whose own affect states are poorly regulated, or who have little or no resilience themselves, may not be able to tolerate these intense and often overwhelming feelings of distress in the infant and rather than providing comfort and re-regulation may become anxious or angry, pushing the infant away, leaving it to cry or handling it roughly. Without the experience of being soothed and returned to calm state, the infant will be unable to monitor and adjust its own feeling states. Rather than experiencing the feeling of emotional validation, that it is okay to feel and to express these feelings, the infant remains unaware of them, cannot discern one from another and will have no point of reference for an emotional self. Only by an attuned response to the feelings we have are we able to bring them into conscious awareness and experience the intimate, healthy emotional connection with others that allows for exploration of our feelings and leads to the development of empathy.

For those infants who are insecurely attached, their experience of the ambivalent mother figure will have been of inconsistent and unpredictable availability from a parent who was preoccupied with themselves, leaving the infant at the mercy of often extreme shifts in feeling states from superficial charm to anger to over-dependence. The mother figure who avoids emotions or who is shut down and unresponsive will have left the infant with feelings of shame for having needs, leading to overt self-reliance which may show itself in an extreme need to care for others coupled with anger at 'self' arising from the shame (McFarlane 2012). Those infants who develop an insecure, disorganised attachment pattern will have experienced the mother figure as frightened herself or frightening to the infant. They will then constantly be checking to see if the environment is safe by closely watching the adult, resulting in hyper-vigilance. Where they have been fearful of parental proximity, they will have internalised a representation of the relationship which is distorted by lack of trust, anger, distress and in extreme cases by terror and fear of annihilation. Perry (2002) suggests that when non-verbal signals are at odds with the verbal message and so do not validate what is being said, the patterns of communication and interaction that will be internalised will be skewed and potentially destructive so that 'a child learns hyper-vigilance. This state of constantly being on guard, ready to fight or to flee and an inability to make and sustain trusting relationships are both characteristic of those young people who schools struggle to contain and who may therefore become disaffected with or excluded from mainstream educational settings'.

So if we have positive early experiences which allow us to develop a secure sense of physical and emotional self, to develop healthy attachments to the significant others in our lives, we are best placed to take on the challenge of our ever-expanding physical, emotional and social world since we do not see it as overtly threatening. Watch a toddler at play outside with their mother figure and you will notice that even as they begin to move away from the adult in exploration of their environment, they will check back physically or visually to ensure that the adult is still available to them. However, they are not anxious, theirs is a secure and healthy attachment and although their preference may be for the mother figure, providing she shows no signs of anxiety around other adults, the infant will also be able to engage with them and begin to increase the circle of attachment. As the infant develops a sense that the world is a safe place and that relationships can be satisfying and fulfilling, they have the secure base that will allow them to spend time with new, strange adults for a short period of time, to engage meaningfully with them and to follow a healthy developmental pathway characterised by engagement in play.

As discussed earlier, Jennings sees play as developing through the three core stages of embodiment, projection and role (EPR).

Within play therapy, this provides us with a framework through which we can gauge a child's progress in regaining both their sense of self and a healthy developmental trajectory. The 'Thrive Approach', developed in 1994 as a response to the rising number and falling age of children excluded from school, provides online 'tools' for assessing the developmental stage of children and young people. It is based on the idea that if children are emotionally thrown off track, they can become stuck at that developmental point so that the resulting behaviour is a communication of unmet or unrecognised need, what Van der Kolk, McFarlane and Weiseath termed 'developmental trauma' (1996).

The Thrive Approach considers that healthy development supports physiological, relational and cognitive regulation systems and comprises six developmental strands or building blocks. As with EPR, we do not progress smoothly from one to the other and may linger in one while stepping into the next, but the key to healthy development is our overall progress through the strands. What play therapy provides children with is the opportunity to go back to the earliest developmental point in order to understand their experiences and find some meaningful resolution for early traumatic or distorted experiences where the gaining of a sense of the body self has been denied. In the Thrive Approach, the strands are as follows, starting at the bottom with 'Being' and emphasising the crucial role our embodied self plays in our development (Figure 3.1).

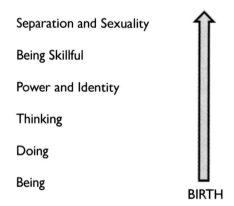

Figure 3.1 The Thrive developmental building blocks

Thrive is widely used by educational settings and stresses that not only is the adult/child relationship the key to the approach, but that it is an under-recognised and under-used resource in schools. From my own educational experience, I would wholeheartedly endorse these sentiments but would also suggest that because our sense of self, our 'being', is dependent on the development of our embodied self, where that relationship takes place is crucial and I would also apply this to play therapy practice. If our embodied self is developed through that early, close and intimate and physical relationship with the mother figure and loaded with sensory experiences, then surely it necessitates physical contact. (This aspect of working is further discussed in Chapter 4.)

Despite my best efforts in providing sand, water, bubbles, clay, soft blankets and beanbags and a host of other sensory toys and activities, including my singing voice, I have never felt that a playroom can provide that rich sensory tapestry that other 'real' environments can supply. Outdoors, we can feel the sun and the wind on our bodies, we can hear the myriad sounds of the trees, birds, creatures, mechanical machines and other human beings who share our space, we can see light and dark in the sky above and feel the texture of the ground beneath us. Within the playroom, children cannot easily explore their physicality with the same freedom to run and jump, to roll and whirl, to experiment with their voice, both real and symbolic by shouting loudly or by screaming, what Santostefano (2004) refers to as 'enact(ing) meanings by expressing vigorous, physical activity and intense emotions in ways that are not typical, certainly for mainstream…therapists' (p.6).

What must always be our guide, however, is the child. If we hold them as central to the process, allowing them to lead the play and trusting that they will know what to do to heal themselves, we can offer an outdoor environment as the connection between the inner and outer worlds and trust them to step out only when and if they are ready to do so. Some may never venture forth, but others, once we have established the containing therapeutic relationship, may want to explore a more a real context and we should feel able to accompany them on their adventure and witness their continued search for meaning.

Symbolic play

From play with the mother figure, social play begins, initially within turn-taking games such as peek-a-boo, but as more active play develops with other attachment figures activity becomes more adventurous, such as rough-and-tumble play with siblings, reminiscent of the play of young animals. Through such demonstrations of our physicality, we develop our understanding of our physical strength, the theme Sherbourne (2001) referred to as 'against'. When they are with peers, children initially play in parallel, in that they may appear to be playing together, but they are each engaged in their own activity, often giving a verbal commentary on their own actions. At this stage, there is no 'to and fro' between the infant and other children, they are sharing the same social space and may be aware of the other's presence, but they are solitary in their play.

> To get the idea of playing, it is helpful to think of the preoccupation that characterizes the playing of a young child. The content does not matter. What matters in the near-withdrawal state akin to the *concentration* of older children and adults. The playing child inhabits an area which cannot easily be left, nor can it easily admit intrusions... It is not inner psychic reality. It is outside the individual, but is not the external world. (Winnicott 1971, p.51)

This is the beginning of the projective stage of the EPR paradigm when children develop symbolic or pretend play. Symbolic play involves the child in play with objects which exist in the real world but are given properties from the child's inner world. It is the externalisation of that inner world, and McMahon (1992) notes that the first real symbolic creation is Winnicott's 'transitional object' (1971), often a soft toy or piece of material which for the infant may represent the safety and security of the mother figure and act as a comfort when she is absent. McMahon goes on to suggest that that this may also be a way for the child to become the mother figure, to internalise her within the infant self.

The early reciprocal play of the to and fro of the attuned mother figure and infant is the first manifestation of imitation which may then develop into play involving imitation of familiar tasks and actions which the child sees happening around the home. Symbolic play first involves familiar objects such as a cup or hat, which the child uses in the everyday way and gradually develops into self-pretend play, where they act out aspects of their everyday activities such as feeding or pretending to sleep. Gradually, toys are incorporated into the play as children start to experiment with familiar roles such as cooking or shopping, building up to more complex scenarios of pretend play where they take on the role of the adult but using toys to play out the scene. This ability to play 'as if' you are the other person, to consider the feelings and experiences of others is what Jennings (2005) calls the dramatic response. It is the precursor to the development of empathy, the ability to stand in someone else's shoes and to know how it feels. Empathy is a key feature of positive, intimate and fulfilling relationships and can only develop as a result of having experienced others' minds as attuned to one's own. As language develops, so children are able to use it to talk about mental states and to recognise and communicate that they and others have needs. Picture the two-year-old whose mother figure is normally happy and sociable but today has a bad headache and so is miserable and less readily responsive. The child, sensing something is amiss, may ask if she is sad or poorly, connecting up her own experience of being nurtured and attended to when she was feeling unwell or out of sorts.

This ability to take on the perspective of another is described as 'theory of mind' and is stronger in those infants who experienced the 'mind-mindedness' (Meins *et al.* 2003) of their attuned mother figure, her acknowledgement of the infant's mental states. In general terms, children understand another's emotions and intentions before they are able to understand thought.

Earlier in the chapter we considered how our earliest memories are embodied or sensory memories arising from the attuned and affirmative relationship with our mother figure. During the development of our embodied self, these memories are pre-verbal, and are stored within our sensory system, Damasio's 'feeling of the feeling' noted at the beginning of this chapter. Music (2011, p.84) calls these early 'biological or physical templates' body-based memories, often referred to as procedural or implicit memories.

In recent years neuroscience has significantly extended our understanding of the brain and its complex functions. McLean's (1990) concept of the triune brain identifies three areas reflecting our evolutionary history:

- the amygdala – contains the brain stem and often referred to as our 'reptilian brain' because it fires our fight, flight or freeze primitive survival response

- the limbic system – our mammalian brain and the area responsible for our emotions and our drive to care for our young and to be social

- the neo-cortex – responsible for executive function, higher order thinking, reasoning, decision making and our conscious experience.

The two cerebral hemispheres of the brain, left and right, have been traditionally seen as having specific functions. The left hemisphere is seen the seat of language and logic while the right hemisphere enables us to be creative, intuitive and emotionally literate. In popular culture, they have been thought of as the male and female brains, an entirely unhelpful delineation that suggests their functions are fixed and independent. They are not, and the two hemisphere are linked by the corpus callosum which facilitates our ability to synthesise the functions and use language to both name and describe an action or a feeling while it is happening. In general terms, the left frontal cortex is the seat of our positive feelings and those who are more typically outgoing, accepting of self and more open to experiences, both positive and negative are more likely to have active left frontal hemispheres (Music 2011). When we perceive ourselves to be in danger, our executive functioning systems close down and our instinctual or survival brain takes over. This can manifest itself as either a hyper-vigilant state where we appear on edge and unable to relax or a dissociative state where we become disconnected from our feelings.

Gerhardt (2004, p.36) notes that our right hemisphere has the capacity to 'grasp the general feel of things' and has a strong link to the orbito-frontal cortex which allows us to manage emotional behaviours and respond to other people's emotional cues. It tells us whether behaviour is socially acceptable and can supress our impulses. It develops after birth and from our social experiences with others. Prolonged neglect, trauma and abuse affect this development as was seen in children who had been placed in orphanages in Eastern Europe where they were denied proper physical care, nurture and meaningful social interactions, resulting in virtual 'black holes' where their orbito-frontal cortex should have been.

From our early mirroring of the familiar activities we see around us, we begin to build up more complex roles to explore as a rehearsal for real life. We have all seen small children playing school, mummies and daddies, shops and hospitals. As our world expands, so does our experience of the roles others play in life and our own repertoire expands, enhanced by the development of our language so that we can narrate our plays, or tell our stories ourselves.

Once our language capacity has developed enough to allow us to create a narrative about events (around the age of two) and our memory systems can encode explicit memories, we can begin to construct our 'autobiographical self'. This depends on us 'having organised memories of situations that characterise our life, such as who our parents are, our names, where we were born…(our likes and dislikes) and our usual reactions to situations' (Music 2011, p.116). These memories locate us in time and in relationship to others but are influenced by our current contexts. Those children who are securely attached tend to have the strongest autobiographical self as their mother figure is likely to have had both the linguistic ability and the narrative style which enables the child to internalise a way of remembering and describing past experiences and events.

Risk and challenge

As we become mobile, we explore our indoor and outdoor environments more fully. From around the age of nine or ten months, my daughter loved to climb. She would pull herself up on the big oak desk we had and onto the sofa beside it. From there she made her way onto its wide arm and up onto the desk. Later, when she was around the age of three, she climbed to the top of the newly installed climbing frame in the garden while I stood at the bottom, heart pounding, encouraging her independence, affirming her bravery and outlining the route down again. Although in one sense I was acutely anxious in case she should fall, I somehow sensed she wouldn't. Her earlier escapades on the desk had shown her to be well co-ordinated with good spatial planning and perhaps my anxiety was a reflection of hers, for although a confident climber, this was a 'first' for her and very much higher than she had ever been before. This illustrates the dilemma for parents in the business of allowing children to take risks. We have to trust them, and we have to trust ourselves with them, to trust that we will know when to call them back and when to let them go. But if we are fearful of risks and challenges ourselves, we are unlikely to develop this level of trust and instead, curtail exploration and diminish their ability to calculate risk for themselves, so putting them in greater danger. Perhaps this is why many therapists would dismiss the idea of moving out of the therapy room, because to do so involves trusting not only the child and the process but oneself as well. We have to be able to face the risk and challenge of the unpredictable and yet continue to hold the space for the child while also remaining connected to our own feelings in order to be fully attuned to the child's processes. If these feelings are predominantly anxiety at or fear of the unexpected, we will be focusing on managing these and so not be fully present for the child. The playroom, seen as the safe, containing space necessary for the child to feel secure enough to step into the unknown, may in reality be safer for the therapist but limit the opportunity for exploration of the full range of embodied experiences of the child. In moving outside, the therapeutic process may therefore be transformed from one where the therapist is in control of events to one where there is a true co-constructed and more democratic relationship between child and therapist which allows for greater freedom and exploration.

If we return to Jennings's idea of circles of care, containment and attachment, I would suggest we might add a fourth element, that of exploration which arises out of the containment and attachment. Initially, infants explore objects within the home, not only toys, but the everyday paraphernalia of the house – utensils, boxes, pets, siblings and all the dusty nooks and crannies we hope no one will investigate too closely. Outside, they are often confined in some other sort of physical 'container': a buggy, a baby bouncer, a lap, a sling or a car. My experience suggests that exploration as a feature of development can be seen through the infant's reaction when placed on the ground on a blanket. Once they are mobile in some way, be it crawling or rolling, they always seem to move to the edge, to set off on their own small adventure! I vividly remember a holiday in Cornwall when my son was first crawling. We sat him on a blanket on the sand next to us with his favourite toys and he immediately crawled off towards the water at an alarmingly rapid pace! He was retrieved and sat once more on the blanket, only to head towards the water again. We took him to the edge and sat him in the shallows, and off he went again, heading into the waves, intent on his own pathway to exploration to facilitate his unique understanding of the world. Although at times it might cause adults anxiety or even inconvenience, we need movement to help us make sense of what we see. Goddard Blythe (2008) writes that:

> Actions carried out in space help us literally to 'make sense' of what we see. Sight combined with balance, movement, hearing, touch and proprioception…help us to integrate sensory experience and can only take place as a result of action and practice. (p.140)

Garner and Bergan (2006) suggest that between the ages of 7 and 12 months, infants' manipulative skills increase to allow both hands to be used in exploration, with patterns of exploratory play emerging between 9 and 16 months showing that they are able to take account of 'visually available surface properties to infer the underlying functional properties of similar objects' (p.5). So if an object is broadly recognisable, previous knowledge and learning about that object is applied. With dissimilar objects, however, exploratory actions are varied as the new objects have no point of reference from previous experience, although actions applied to them will have. From 9 to 12 months, much play relates to developing physical skills and Garner and Bergan further note that infants experience their physicality by 'learning to pull themselves up, cruise along furniture, stand alone and (for some) walk independently' (p.6). However, our physical abilities are likely to differ depending on factors such as genetics, our body structure and build and the experience of differing environments available to us.

As well as making sense of previous experience, movement and exploration provide us with challenge and the opportunity to take risks and experiment with our developing physicality knowing that our mother or other attachment figure will be there, to attend to us. Montessori considered development as occurring in three stages characterised by flexible age bands:

- the absorbent mind: conception to 6 years (with 0–3 being unconscious absorbent and 3–6 conscious absorbent)
- childhood: 6–12 years
- adolescence: 12–18 years.

She felt that the absorbent mind stage was critical to human development, with the fundamental principle being that the child was a spontaneous learner, driven by an inner need to learn from the environment through active learning and exploration. She also believed that this environment should support the development of the whole child and must above all be safe (Isaacs 2007). As our early relationship develops the mother figure, although still attuned to the infant's needs, finds herself adapting less readily. This occurs because usual routines and activities within the household eventually need to resume, although they now accommodate the new being. The infant may have to wait just a few more minutes before being picked up or fed. The omnipotent self is questioned but because the mother figure has consistently responded in the past, the infant can tolerate this and remain confident that their needs will be met. If the infant is left for too long, they may begin to feel that the mother figure is no longer available to them and become fearful and unwilling to take a risk. A continuing sense of omnipotence is likely to leave the infant feeling that there is nothing they can't do so that even the smallest of setbacks can diminish their sense of competency and leave them unwilling to risk failure and therefore unadventurous and unwilling to explore.

In Chapter 2, we considered the idea that within society we appear to have come to view children as vulnerable and constantly at risk and therefore for many this vital stage of exploration, challenge and risk taking can be curtailed by several things: loss of both urban and rural play spaces, parental concern for safety, increased amounts of time spent indoors on screen-based activities and loss of PE and sports time from school curricula. But facing a challenge, taking a personal risk in a safe environment, one where the benefits of the risk have been weighed against the likelihood of actual harm, is good for us. It supports the further development of our body self and builds a sense of personal confidence and skilfulness. We grow to see ourselves as capable and competent, able to look after ourselves and others and able to calculate risk for ourselves. However, therapists may see the environments outside the playroom as not offering the security and stability children often seek when they are anxious or distressed. Within the therapeutic alliance (discussed further in Chapter 4), it is the very presence of the therapist which provides the 'walls', the containment and security needed to anchor children in therapy. It is in the space between us that the play occurs and even within a fixed indoor space, that space can expand and contract in a way that is reminiscent of the pulsating, rhythmical qualities of our bodies. If we move outside, we can still maintain those symbolic walls (Figure 3.2) and, if needed, can provide smaller, more intimate spaces, either through those which occur naturally or those which have been constructed as shown in the photographs in Part II.

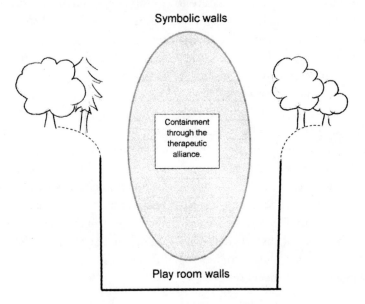

Figure 3.2 Containment through symbolic walls

Tovey (2007) discusses how as children, we often construct activities which hover on the borderline between safe and unsafe. I remember as a child, going out across the fields in winter with a gang of friends and finding that the snow had drifted deeply against the feet of the pylons. We found one which had particularly deep falls and spent a happy afternoon daring each other to climb higher onto the metalwork and jump off into the snow. Another time, with the same group of friends, we tried to climb on the backs of the cows corralled in a small enclosure in one of the nearby fields. Perhaps it is the excitement of the play which feeds our feelings of exhilaration, reminding us of our physical capabilities and letting us know that we are in charge of our body but can also take a risk with it by testing out our competence and capabilities. I am not suggesting that the therapist constructs risky activities of such magnitude, or indeed constructs anything at all. But to offer the opportunity to explore fully the limits of our body in the pursuit of understanding ourselves, our immediate world and the connection between the two would seem to me only to strengthen our feelings of autonomy and agency. Tovey concludes that what we need to be offering, is not environments safe '*from* all possible harm, (but those which) offer(s) safety to explore, experiment, try things out and to take risks' (p.102). If we can trust children and support them when they are ready to test themselves within the safety of the therapeutic alliance, then we give them a different experience of being scared, where instead of being the victim, they are in charge, can exert power and control and can shape the ending, be competent and skilful and develop a sense of body self that is theirs and not one imposed on them by others. We need this reminder so that we may feel confident about and at home in our bodies, for, as was discussed in Chapter 2, there is today a strong sexualised component to much of the media material connected with bodies. We need to offer children and young people the chance to reconnect with their bodies and to have a different relationship with them which does not distort their sense of self, shatter their wholeness or disempower them from being different and celebrating their uniqueness and diversity.

Developing 'place' attachment

Outdoor environments also offer first-hand experiences of transformation as described earlier in the work of the Penn Green Centre. Weather changes transform dry mud into a sticky goo, water into ice, a clear view into a grey fog. These concrete experiences offer children first-hand knowledge and understanding of the concept of cause and effect and of how some things change forever and some return again to their original form, much as our lived experiences and relationships do. In my work as a specialist advisory teacher, some of our most troubled and troubling young people accessed Forest School and as a result seemed to 'improve'. That is, they appeared to be calmer and more relaxed and therefore better able to sustain relationships with both adults and peers (as in Chapter 1). The inability to make and sustain satisfying and fulfilling relationships within home and school was the common feature of the young people's presenting difficulties. The staff they were working with at Forest School were adept at making positive relationships but what I often noticed was that the thing which initially sparked the children's enthusiasm was *where* they were going – to the woods – and what they were physically doing in the form of activities. They were demonstrating a growing relationship with the physical space, a connection to the woods themselves. It seemed to me that for them, with their history of inconsistent and often chaotic family and school relationships, the woods had become the object of their attachment since it was constant in its form, reliable, in that it was always there waiting to 'attend' to their needs and trustworthy in that it was accepting of who they were, offering itself to them to meet their needs and yet waiting to be manipulated by them in order that they might better understand themselves. It was an equal relationship.

A study of the key worker role within the charity Kids Company (Lemma 2010), which works with some of society's most traumatised young people, found that the first relationship they were likely to make was with the physical space that was offered as a shelter to them. It became their first attachment, 'a space to be or place to hang out' (p.412); somewhere which provided continuity and stability and a feeling of safety which Lemma notes has been described as the 'brick mother' by Rey (1994). Jack (2010) suggests that the 'feel of a place' takes longer to develop than familiarity with its physical properties and is dependent on everyday rituals, routines and activities which invest a place with personal meaning. It is the quality of the experience that is important, rather than the length of time spent there. The environmental psychology movement describes this attachment to an environment as 'place attachment' where a physical environment also has symbolic meaning and evokes emotions, giving us a sense of containment and security like that of the attuned mother figure. It can provide us with a new template for relationship building which transcends our previous distorted experiences.

Just as the infant who is disconnected from their mother figure will struggle to connect to their own experiences in any meaningful way, perhaps our disconnection from the land around us, our lack of place attachment in broader society, is what often leaves us struggling to maintain meaningful relationships within our communities. Offering children who come to play therapy an opportunity to access outdoor environments would seem therefore to offer greater potential for developing a secure sense of autonomous, competent and skilful self and a stable and sustainable relationship with a 'nature mother', one who will reliably be there throughout their lifespan to offer security and comfort and meaningful restorative connection. Through the changes in nature they can experience real transformation even as they undergo this same process for themselves and can see the possibility for change within.

> Nature offers healing for a child living in a destructive family or neighbourhood. Given a chance, a child will bring the confusion of the world to the woods, wash it in the creek, (and) turn it over to see what lives on the unseen side of that confusion. In nature a child finds freedom, fantasy and privacy: a place distant from the adult world, a separate peace. (Louv 2005, p.7)

Chapter 4

Connecting with the 'Nature Mother'

This chapter will set out to allay therapist anxieties about leaving the playroom by discussing the idea of symbolic 'walls' to offer containment through the therapeutic relationship and to create the safe therapeutic space. It will consider the therapeutic alliance and power issues that might arise within it, and strengthen the concept of the 'nature mother' as a potential third element in the therapeutic relationship.

In the previous chapter the term 'nature mother' was used to describe how the natural environment can take on the role of a mother figure, engendering feelings of security and containment through its permanence, availability, challenge and possibilities for creativity and transformation.

> 'When I'm in the woods,' she said, 'I feel like I'm in my mother's shoes... Sometimes I go there when I'm mad – and then, just with the peacefulness I'm better. I can come back home happy, and my Mom doesn't even know why.' (Louv 2010, p.13)

This place attachment supports the development of resilience, 'the mental, emotional and physical fortitude to recover from adversity and realize potential' (Nature Nurture 2011). This is one of the key outcomes from play therapy and depends on the child having a secure sense of self, including body self as discussed previously. To me the outdoors seems a natural extension of the playroom but I realise that for many other therapists there may be issues around confidentiality and the holding of the safe space, which I will explore here. Although it is not my intention to convince you that I am right, I feel that some therapeutic traditions, rather than enhancing the client's experience, can be upheld in order that *we* feel secure and we need to have a dynamic approach to practice which reflects our own curiosity and thirst for learning and developing in parallel with our clients' processes. We should be doing what we do because we have looked at the needs of our clients, the experiences they bring and those we have created together and have used these to inform, shape and develop practice. Doing something just because we have always done it that way is no reason for not changing.

When I trained to be a non-directive play therapist, I carried out my 'clinical practice' in schools, which are generally by their very nature, structured and well organised. However, they are also fluid and dynamic, particularly where timetabling and room allocation are concerned. Those of you who have worked in them in any capacity will know that in order to respond to the needs of the whole school community, including governors, parents, local authority support staff and children in crisis, what was to be at the end of the previous day may well have changed the next morning. My personal experience is that however many times you remind staff that you are not to be interrupted, put notices on the door to say that play therapy is in progress or speak directly to anyone who has the audacity to come into your session, there are still times when someone 'urgently' needs something in the room you have been given, or needs to 'just let you know' some snippet of information about the child you are with.

I was working with an 11-year-old client, and the time of our session had to be moved from before lunch to before the morning break. This resulted in a peer from his class being dispatched by the teacher to bring him his snack since our new session finished just as snacks were being served. It posed a real dilemma – routine and structure of the day and therefore the time of the snack were imperative to the ethos of the school which took boys from generally chaotic environments. The food was important for my client to see him through the busy morning sessions, but the interruption could have been seen as breaching confidentiality. My client had been open with both his peers and the staff about the 'art teacher' he worked with and through discussion, and at his suggestion, we agreed to end his session five minutes early to allow for the snack to be delivered as he felt more comfortable with having someone come to the door than he would if he had to eat his snack alone. I received the food at the door on his behalf and gently fielded any enquiries about what we were doing with a simple 'some artwork'. Although there might have been other solutions which would not have had an impact on the existing structure of the session, I felt my client's autonomy and integrity were maintained as he had come up with his own solution to the problem and had felt confident in coping with the interruption, both of these being indicative of strengthening resilience and emotional competence.

However, when I was completing my training, it was suggested that any such breaches of the confidentiality of the session should be vigorously repelled in a manner which was very dramatic in its demonstration. It appeared to involve raising one's voice to the 'visitor' and forcefully closing the door to them while making it very clear that they had committed a heinous and thoughtless transgression. I felt that all this was likely to do was compromise the therapeutic relationship by showing the therapist to be unable to manage effectively their own emotions, and to mimic the same sort of uncontrolled adult behaviour the client might well have experienced previously. This was likely to make them feel much more unsafe than if the visitor had been quietly told that 'now is not a good time' and gently steered back out through the door with a clear reminder that the session should not be interrupted in the future. Adults modelling how to manage their feelings in an appropriate way is surely imperative for the development of healthy self-management in children and young people. In order to begin to explore why we might challenge the prevailing view that the only truly 'safe' space is the playroom, we need to consider the purpose of therapy for children.

The British Association of Play Therapy (BAPT) gives its theoretical definition of play therapy as:

> The dynamic process between child and Play Therapist in which the child explores at his or her own pace and with his or her own agenda those issues, past and current, conscious and unconscious, that are affecting the child's life in the present. The child's inner resources are enabled by the therapeutic alliance to bring about growth and change. Play Therapy

is child-centred, in which play is the primary medium and speech is the secondary medium. (BAPT 2011)

Axline (1969) defines it as:

> based upon the fact that play is the child's natural medium of self-expression. It is an opportunity which is given to the child to 'play out his feeling and problems. (p.9)

Cattananch (2003) notes that within play therapy there is:

> the central assumption that play is the place where children first recognise the separateness of what is 'me' and 'not me' and begin to develop a relationship with the world beyond the self. It is the child's way of making contact with their environment. (p.24)

Writing in *The Handbook of Play Therapy* (1992, p.7), McMahon notes that 'the aim of play therapy is to repair the process of attachment and containment' and Daniels, in *Processes in the Arts Therapies* (1999), suggests that play therapy requires two key elements – the safe space and the therapist's presence – which together facilitate the telling of the child's story, regardless of the toys and resources available.

From these definitions emerge some primary areas of focus through which we may take a closer look at how the process of play therapy, in which the therapist is the facilitator of change, can then be further explored with a view to considering moving into the outdoors:

- the therapeutic alliance
- the use of the child's inner resources
- working through play
- the safe space.

The therapeutic alliance

Writing in *Trauma and Recovery* (2001), Lewis Herman notes that 'the core experiences of psychological trauma are disempowerment and disconnection from others', and suggests that '(since) recovery...

is based on the need for empowerment and…the creation of new connections, (it) can take place only in the context of relationships'. However, relationships are complex and she further notes that recovery necessitates the re-creation of damaged psychological faculties that, when healthy, give us 'basic capacities for trust, competence, autonomy, initiative, identity and intimacy' (p.133).

It is difficult to set any one of these against the other in terms of the importance to relationship building, for without a clear sense of our own identity we will not develop autonomy and may remain dependent or dislocated in new relationships. Without autonomy, we cannot take initiative and it is likely that our sense of personal competence will be impaired, leaving us unsure of our abilities to make and sustain healthy connections with others. Without trust, true intimacy that nourishes and sustains relationships is impossible and so we can see the interdependency of each of these fragile faculties. However, trust is central to the formation of new relationships and critical for the child coming to therapy whose previous experience of relationships is likely to have been very damaging.

I see the therapeutic alliance as a meeting between the attuned, empathic and accepting adult and the child who knows instinctively how they can repair the damage that has been done to them, and recognises in the adult one to whom they can entrust themselves and who will accompany them on their exploration as enabler and co-explorer (West 1992). It facilitates an appropriate and healthy emotional bond where the purpose of the therapy is recognised by both but may be explicitly spoken by neither and it allows for therapeutic progress of the child. The relationship between the therapist and child results in the creation of symbolic walls, the container, as the arms of the mother contain the child and it encompasses what Winnicott describes as 'the playground…(the) potential space between the mother and the baby or joining the mother and baby' (1971, p.47). It could therefore be thought of as 'transportable', such as to an outdoor, more natural space.

One of the most powerful therapy sessions I had with a child took place in a field at the edge of the woods where she and her group had gone on their weekly Forest School visit. There were six children altogether, including the girl I was working with, all five or six years old with profound or multiple learning needs. There were five adults with us, including the Forest School leader, and we had walked through the woods to the field. Sammy and I had been working together for over a year and were a little distance away from the others, near a hedge. She was sitting and I was facing her, kneeling low into the grass so our faces were level. In the moments that followed, the intensity of the therapeutic alliance was such that it emphasised the existence of symbolic walls – an invisible container for both the work and for us, together in that green space. Around us children played, adults chatted with them and with each other and we were oblivious to it all. My sense of attunement to Sammy was perhaps the strongest it had ever been and it was this that I believe allowed for that sense of being completely within a contained space, contained by the alliance between us, and paradoxically, by being in an 'open' natural space with the ritual of our interaction creating the 'playground'. It was a warm day and there was a breeze blowing. The grass made a cushion to the earth and with the noise of the others in the distance this all provided a rich sensory tapestry which surrounded us, enhancing the sense of a safe space. It was as if we were in a triadic rather than dyadic relationship – Sammy, me and 'nature mother', the land around us, in equal partnership. We stayed like this for some 15 minutes or so and then Sammy got up, went to a large, clear puddle near the gate into the field and putting her face right into the water, came up blowing like a horse and laughing! Something had shifted and the whole experience had been truly mindful – in the moment – for both of us.

Axline's (1969) eight guiding principles of non-directive play therapy incorporate the core conditions of Rogerian psychotherapy which Wilson, Kendrick and Ryan (1992) describe as genuineness and authenticity, non-possessive warmth and accurate empathy. Her first principle tells us that the therapist must develop a warm, friendly relationship with the child, in which a good rapport is established as soon as possible. Asked what I did to build a relationship so quickly with children whose experience of adults has more often than not been negative, I could only think that it was a case of 'unconscious competence' in that I was unable to say exactly how this happened, although it often seems to take no time at all for children to establish a relationship which allows them to get the sessions underway and to engage in therapeutic play. On reflection, I think that it is not about identifying skills we have and that we might teach someone, for implicit in having to teach them, the notion of authenticity and genuineness already seems comprised. It is more a case of who we are, the sum of our life experiences. Alice Miller writes about this in her book *The Drama of Being a Child* (1997). In discussing why 'we' might become psychotherapists, she suggests that a likely personal history of being children whose own needs went unmet in order to fulfil the needs of others to gain acceptance and love, has given us the powerful antennae we use to respond to our clients. However, she also notes that unless we recognise this and have taken steps to 'live with the reality of our past' (p.23), we are in danger of remaining unaware of these unconscious feelings which will then impact on our work with clients. So, most of all, perhaps being the attuned therapist, able to establish and maintain the therapeutic alliance, is about being congruent and authentic, since children are very adept at spotting the lack of these qualities. As therapists, we need to be able to 'sit with' the child's most difficult and potentially overwhelming feelings and to 'hold' the space, that is to say provide containment, wherever that space may be.

> Even though the emotions expressed in play therapy are often expressed via symbol or metaphor, the emotions are still there, benefitting from our witnessing them. It is our presence in the play experience that makes it therapeutic. (McCarthy 2012, p.29)

To hold the space effectively means having to address our shadow side; to be aware of what we are bringing into the session. If it is our own fears, anxieties and frailties which are just beyond our peripheral vision and which occupy our thoughts, it may be that our clients stories will leave us in turmoil and unable to be present to witness their experiences. This counter transference, our 'emotions, thoughts and behaviour arising from past baggage' can be identified through the supervision process and may need to be taken to personal theapy so we can ensure they do not interfere with our work (West 1992, p.1691). To develop the reflexive capacity crucial to facilitating change, we must look inside ourselves and see the hurt child we perhaps once were and acknowledge her presence and the connection she allows us to make with the children with whom we work today.

In describing what he calls the art of the therapeutic relationship, Landreth (2002) tells us that the therapist needs to be open-minded and sensitive to the child's world and that effective play therapists are personally secure, able to recognise and accept personal limitations. Furthermore, he notes that 'all therapists need self-understanding and insight into their own motivations, needs, blind spots, biases, personal conflicts and areas of emotional difficulty as well as personal strengths' (p.102). Without this depth of self-reflection and awareness, we are unlikely to be able to connect with these same dimensions within the child and our own needs and desires may emerge in ways which control and limit the creative exploration of the child.

If we are to create a productive therapeutic alliance, which allows for transformation, then we need to have respect for and trust in both our clients' processes and our own. We need a commitment to being honest and genuine, to being sincere, and we need integrity to act wholly and soundly towards both ourselves and our clients. Above all, we need to have the courage to use what we know and understand, what we have learned and what we believe in order to give our clients the best therapeutic opportunities (BAPT 2008). To do this authentically, with the child held as central to the process, may challenge us. However, if we never reflect on the 'why' or 'how' of what we do or consider why we believe what we do, then the therapeutic process we construct with the child will be static and imbued with our own unconscious feelings and needs and limit the child's creativity and potential for change.

I recognise that moving outside the playroom, long held as the 'holy temple within which therapy should take place' (Santostefano 2004, p.6) will pose a real dilemma for many therapists. One of my colleagues asked me how, if working in a public space, I could protect the child from the unpredictable. However, surely the unpredictable is an integral part of the therapeutic process? As the therapist in the room, we can never be sure what will arise, even within the security of the closed playroom. Rather than protecting the child and making everything right, the play therapist can use the unpredictable in what McCarthy (2012) calls 'provocation'. He suggests that provocation occurs 'from within the playing child and the creative experience' so that children often compose play situations which give validation to their thinking only to disrupt them but respond playfully to the resulting creations. Where the child is unable to play or is stuck in a rigid routine so that they require help to access a deeper and more dynamic level then the therapist may need to be provocative, to indirectly give the child permission to play through their own playfulness.

The engaged play therapy process is one of an ongoing unsettling, if it is allowed to be. This may be why so many therapists attempt to control things by not allowing spontaneous play. It disturbs the equilibrium and challenges stasis (McCarthy 2012). By responding to the unexpected event in a playful way, the therapist reduces the child's anxiety and frees them up to participate in finding a resolution. Should the unexpected be potentially harmful, then the therapist may need to apply new limits based on what is needed therapeutically for the child at that moment. In discussing working outdoors with adult clients, Jordan and Marshall (2010, p.352) describe this process as 'fluid contracting', necessary as the client and the therapist face the outdoor terrain and all the resultant challenges.

The unpredictability of the natural environment is, however, one of its great strengths. It characterises life experiences and can be very energising when experienced from within the safety of the therapeutic alliance. It offers concrete examples of transformation (see Chapter 3) and has aspects symbolic of the rhythmic and pulsating nature of our emotional responses. Picture a stormy day with the waves crashing onto the rocks and spray flying into the air – a vivid metaphor for anger, rolling uncontrollably in a forceful wave, washing over us and spilling beyond us to touch others. Yet later, sometimes even on the same day, the waves have lost their potency, the anger has been discharged, has dissipated, the sea is transformed and some measure of calm is restored. The child who has felt anger but has never experienced being soothed by the mother figure may run shrieking out of reach of the spray, overwhelmed by embodied feelings of anxiety or fright that they may be swept up and bowled over. Gently caught by the therapist, the child experiences not only the physical containment but is held within the security of the therapeutic relationship. Their fears are calmed and they can achieve stasis just as they would have done with an attuned mother figure. When the sea changes, the child sees at first hand the possibility for transformation. They have experienced all of this through their very being, through all of their senses, enabling the creation of a new and healthier embodied self.

> Enacting embodied life – metaphors…has the most power to resolve the impact of trauma and promote change. I conceptualize a child's self to include the meanings the child has given to experiences with human and non-human environments with which…(they have) interacted… Enacting embodied meanings…is necessary to resolve at the embodied level the impact that is interfering with the child's development. (Santostefano 2004, pp.6–7)

As a child begins to explore further from the attuned mother figure, boundaries become necessary for both physical safekeeping and for continuing emotional containment. Within the therapeutic alliance, boundary or limit setting is an integral part of building the feeling of safety and containment but perhaps because the very heart of the non-directive approach is permissiveness, limits or boundaries might seem to be the very antithesis of this. Boundaries serve to help the child learn how to limit their own reactions and learn self-control through having a choice in the action they take, rather than complying with someone else's idea of what is right. Landreth (2002) notes that limit setting should be based on sound principles and clear and definable criteria so that it enhances the therapeutic relationship and facilitates psychological growth. Growth cannot be achieved when anxiety, guilt or shame are present. If the child is permitted to hurt themselves or the therapist, or damage the playroom, toys and resources, then these negative feelings are likely to appear. However, limits can be minimal and given only when the need arises, rather than forming a potential barrier to experimentation and creativity when laid out specifically within the first session. We can tell a child that our 'job' is to keep them safe but they will know this intuitively if we are accepting of ourselves and open to and accepting of them so that they experience us as genuine, congruent and authentic. Limits are necessary in order to create feelings of safety and security for the child and to promote the well-being of the therapist. A therapist will not be truly present for the child if they are concerned for their own physical safety or concerned about what the child's play might involve. We need to be secure in ourselves and to know that we can deal with whatever arises, not by putting a list of 'rules' on the wall but by having confidence in our ability to meet the unexpected and set appropriate limits which maintain safety and security and keep the child connected to reality, to the 'here and now'. Landreth (2002, p.254) tells us that 'when the therapist states a limit to protect herself from harm, (her) personhood and respect for herself are declared. At that moment, the experience with the child truly becomes a living relationship anchored in the dynamics of the process of the reality of the moment'.

If we move out of the playroom, we can still maintain feelings of safety and security because the therapeutic relationship in its totality will still exist. The limits we have set within the playroom apply outside for it is no more appropriate to cover the exterior walls with paint or destroy the natural environment than it is to wreck the playroom and all the resources and toys therein.

If the thought of leaving the security of the playroom provokes feelings of intense anxiety in the therapist then the play needs to remain contained indoors but the source of the anxiety requires exploration. If it is connected with a need to feel in control then this must be addressed through supervision or personal therapy since it suggests that the therapeutic relationship is hindered by power issues. Berger (2006, in Jordan and Marshall 2010) recognises these issues as inherent in the physical setting for therapy, suggesting that the more traditional room can be seen as set up, controlled and owned by the therapist, so creating a power imbalance. If what happens in the room has to be controlled by the therapist then the therapist's own needs are being put before the child's, and since the very essence of the non-directive approach is the permissiveness, this will be compromised by such issues. How can we expect our clients to develop trust in us to hold the space and keep them safe and secure when we cannot trust ourselves to do the same?

The child's inner resources

Discussing the Danish Forest School approach, Williams-Siegfredson (2012) tells us that the Danish pedagogical approach to early years education focuses on the interaction of two key elements: the human beings both adult and child and the physical environment whether indoors or outdoors. Within this, the outdoor environment is seen as a continuous and integrated element of practice. This approach to learning can be described as holistic in that it aims to support the development of physical, psychological and aesthetic aspects of the child and key elements in this approach are risk taking and challenge (see Chapter 3) in which the child is supported by the 'pedagogue'. This is not dissimilar to West's 'whole child' description of play therapy given earlier. So if the process of play therapy can benefit all aspects of a child's development, could it be that they bring all of these parts to bear on the therapeutic process?

Egan (2002) describes the 'helping' relationship as a working alliance in which both the helper and the client work together, deploying their confidence in each other and their motivation for change in a process which also relies on quality engagement with each other. Through the therapeutic alliance, trust is established that can allow the child to begin to access all available inner resources, which may be limited at first but increase as their journey through therapy progresses and they gain a stronger sense of self. So what might these inner resources be?

When I was working with Hannah, a seven-year-old girl, excluded from her community school and placed in a pupil referral unit, I recognised in her a core physicality that seemed to be her very essence. It was as if all other aspects of her self had been stripped away or used up in the very act of surviving within a neglectful and dysfunctional family who had left her, at the age of three, wandering the streets in a dirty nappy in search of food.

Although the term neglect is very difficult to define, the NSPCC (2011) suggests that failure to do the following can be considered as neglectful:

- provide adequate food, clothing and shelter

- protect a child from physical and emotional harm or danger

- provide adequate supervision

- ensure access to medical care or treatment when needed

- respond to a child's emotional needs.

This correlates well with Maslow's hierarchy of needs, the first and therefore most critical of which are physiological – breathing, food water, warmth, sleep, sex, excretion and homeostasis – with the next level being safety and security needs. Without these most basic aspects of our physical survival needs being met, our sense of being important, of having worth, never develops and our sense of body self is severely comprised.

Hannah had been excluded for verbal abuse and physically aggressive responses to both adults and her peers. During our sessions, she responded to any interaction from me with a request that I zip my mouth, something she had been unable to do in school herself. Her early embodied experiences had left her with no 'voice' and within her family she had learned that the more loud and aggressive your voice was, the more in control you could be and the more your needs were met. When she arrived at her first school, highly anxious, unprepared and in a permanent state of hyper-arousal she used her experiences to gain a sense of control by replicating what she had seen. Constantly responding from the earliest, instinctual area of the brain, rather than flee or freeze, she fought, hurting both adults and her peers.

In relation to her early and traumatic experiences, if we return to Lewis Herman's (2001) core psychological faculties of healthy development – trust, competence, autonomy, initiative, identity and intimacy – what had been compromised by Hannah's experiences were trust, identity and intimacy. However, her survival had necessitated initiative to seek out food, and she had acted autonomously – independently and on her own behalf – and had been competent in her ability to survive. So there is something of a paradox here since, as McFarlane (2012) recognises, neglect *can* create resilience. The attributes we use to survive in adversity are what therapy aims to develop to aid our process of recovery, although they need to be re-configured in a developmentally healthy way that enables relationships to form.

In her neglectful and aggressive family, Hannah's sense of body self had not been developed in a healthy way but her experience of caring for herself had given her this core physicality.

Yet during a traumatic event, it is this very physicality or what Lewis Herman describes as our 'bodily integrity' (2001, p.33) that is threatened by the event. So here again is a paradox. When our physical self is threatened, it is our physical responses – fight, flight or freeze – which aid our very survival. The arousal or hyper-arousal we experience in response to stress is regulated by the limbic system in the brain which evaluates a situation and signals to our autonomic nervous system (ANS) to prepare either to rest or to expend energy. The ANS regulates our heart and circulatory systems, our breathing, the movement of our muscles, the dilation of our pupils and the functions of our intestines, bowels and bladder. These are our visceral functions, the basis of our physicality (Rothschild 2000). So in relation to the therapeutic healing process, what we bring is our physical self – that is, our most basic resource – and from it our fuller sense of self can develop. However, as we have already noted in Chapter 3, traumatic experiences are likely to have left us with a distorted sense of our body or perhaps even no real sense of it all.

We will all encounter stressful situations in our lives and most of us will have developed ways of coping that enable us to meet adversity without it annihilating our sense of self. Hannah's experiences were much more destructive and therefore their impact was far longer lasting.

Rothschild (2000) discusses four types of stress. First, that which many of us may experience as the response to negative situations or those events which we choose, but which may temporarily place unusual demands on us, such as moving house. Second, a much more extreme response to stress which results from a traumatic experience – traumatic stress, which in turn can lead to post-traumatic stress (PTS) where symptoms persist after the event. For a percentage of those experiencing PTS, the symptoms become so pervasive that they lead to 'loss at a severe and serious level... loss of self-worth, self-respect, meaning of life and faith' (Winn 2008, p.3) and result in post-traumatic stress disorder (PTSD). Young Minds (2013), in discussing the issue of post-traumatic stress, suggests that a traumatic experience is an event that continues to exert negative effects on thinking (cognition), feelings (affects) and behaviour long after the event is in the past. It is worse if the traumatic event happened at an early age, was caused by a parent or carer, went on for a long time and was severe.

Berger and Lahad (2013) in discussing PTSD note that:

> The behaviour of a child who is exhibiting some of the more aggressive and violent aspects of the disorder may be interpreted simplistically as violent or lacking in discipline...and her behaviour can dramatically influence the entire class (so that the teacher)...may respond with educational punishments...unhelpful to the child. (p.20)

This had been Hannah's story.

Alice Miller, writing in *The Drama of Being a Child* (1997, p.122), suggests that 'the aim of therapy...is not to correct the past, but to enable the patient both to confront his own history and grieve over it...becom(ing) consciously aware of his parents' unconscious manipulation and contempt, so that he can free himself from them'. After years of being bombarded by loud and often out of control voices which raged at and frightened her, demeaned her and constantly told her she had got it wrong, Hannah's request to me to be silent was symbolic of her need to shut out her own voice, the one she experienced as causing rejection and dislocation and the demanding and bombarding voices of adults both at home and at school. This was the first time she had been able to control a grown-up's voice, and in doing so she began the process of freeing herself, and of finding a new, more productive and empowered voice for herself.

The therapeutic process for children is facilitated through their use of symbolic, imaginative and dramatic play. They bring their creativity to us and in so doing, unlock their potential for change. The use of symbol and metaphor to explore past experiences, to rework them and to find resolution in new meaning enables access to the unconscious, bringing it into awareness so that the symbol provides a bridge between their inner and outer worlds. These symbols, each one standing for something other than itself, are the unspoken 'language' of the play and while there may be some universal interpretations of this symbolic language, it is crucial for the therapist to accept the child's symbols as unique to them in the context of the moment of play in which they occur. When we are accepting of them through our permissiveness and openness to the child's play and use them in our responses, then symbols can communicate experiences which are too complex, frightening or overwhelming to be put into words, even if the child's language development allowed for this. They allow for the child to play as if they were something or someone else, to take on a role. Jennings (2011) has described this as the dramatic response which arises from the early rhythmic, sensory and dramatic actions between the infant and the mother figure as they play as if they were the other. Through the playing of roles and the use of symbol and metaphor, children can 'speak' about traumatic events, and although 'they may be depicting horrors, they are simultaneously playing with what is depicted (so that) play is both an act of creativity and discovery. This can allow the residual effects of the trauma in their psyches and bodies to resolve in the very same play' (McCarthy 2012, p.29).

In order to free up their creativity, our clients need to trust us, to experience us as reliable, authentic and congruent. For children who have experienced abusive relationships with adults on whom they should have been able to depend to keep them safe, it may take many, many months and even years before they can begin to trust and so form new meaningful relationships that will be sustained. Sensitive attunement in our early relationship with our mother figure teaches us that we will be attended to, builds a sense of trust of present relationships and hope for the same qualities in future ones. As Erikson (1995) notes in discussing our most important developmental stage of trust versus mistrust, it is not the quantities of what is on offer from the mother figure, but the quality of the relationship which is important in establishing trust. Where adults do not provide the care and containment we need to ensure we feel secure and safe, we experience not only a loss of this trust but also a loss of belief that we are loveable and of worth. The loss of trust is threefold: a loss of trust in others, a loss of trust in ourselves as having worth and an inability to trust others with ourselves. By accepting the child exactly as they are, and by allowing them to lead the way in the play, the therapist creates a sense of a trusted self in the child, 'a sense of being "all right", of being oneself and of becoming what other people trust she will become' (Erikson 1995, p.234). How we are with the child; the quality of the therapeutic alliance we create with them will determine how much trust they can place in us and the efficacy of the play therapy process.

Working through play – attending to our own playfulness

Earlier in this chapter I noted the central role of symbolic play in the therapeutic process and in Chapter 3 discussed how play develops from the early attuned interactions between the mother figure and the infant through the three broad stages of embodiment, projection and role. What is crucial in these early stages is the ability of the mother figure to be playful herself and this is also true of the play therapist. To enable the playfulness of clients, we too must demonstrate our ability to be so. If permissiveness is imbued with our own discomfort with mess and noise or our feeling of being overwhelmed by big, energetic physical activities then we may inadvertently curb the playfulness in the children we are working with. Earlier in the chapter I considered the need for us to look inside ourselves to see how what we are experiencing might be impacting on the therapeutic process, and included in this is our own ability to respond with genuine playfulness. If we are not playful in other areas of our lives then what we may bring to the playroom is a constructed playfulness that lacks congruence and authenticity, something that we slip into before the session and cast off after the child has gone. Our own playfulness is just as dependent on early experiences as our client's will be and we need to reflect on any limitations to this aspect of our practice through supervision and personal therapy.

As adults, our playfulness can be thwarted by the everyday stresses and strains inherent in managing busy schedules of work, life and family. Our education system consigns play to the early years of pre-school and the Foundation Stage of formal schooling. Rarely are free play opportunities extended into Key Stages 2 and 3 (ages 7–14) except during organised PE and games lessons and at break times when there may be restrictions due to space and numbers. Much of our leisure time is in the form of constructed, organised and risk-free activities and this is extending more and more to our children, as discussed in Chapter 2.

The therapeutic training I have done with adults almost always includes practical activities to provide experiential learning – the opportunity to know what it is like to be our clients. On a recent training day I was asked to deliver a session on messy play to some experienced play and drama therapists. The practical element involved each therapist having a small bowl of dry sand. After some guided input to get to know the properties of the sand, the participants were encouraged to add water to it and observe the changes. At first, several were tentative, adding just a small amount of fluid, with some preferring to continue with a soft dry texture and adding none. Gradually, by my being provocative and adding more water to my own bowl, playfully mixing and splatting it, the others seemed encouraged to do the same. Then I suggested we might put all our sand together in the middle of a large waterproof ground sheet to see if we might create a shared image. Some preferred to keep their own separate initially, while others added theirs willingly to the messy pile in the middle. Eventually all the sand was added and we began to mix and swirl the mess. Then someone said, 'I feel like I want to get a handful and throw it down'. So we took a collective risk and prepared for the challenge! The more we threw it down, the bolder the throwing became until it was splattering our arms and clothes. Then we started to smooth it on the backs of our hands and on the hands of those near us as if our playful children within had been unleashed. Even though the session had started with a short, focused and directed activity, playfulness prevailed. What was interesting in the discussion afterwards was the responsibility some had felt initially for not getting wet sand on the floor of the room, for not making a mess – a reflection, they felt, of their early experiences as children who had to be tidy and clean or of their therapeutic role as the holder and cleaner of the mess.

For most of us, that playfulness is inherent within us, even if it has been buried by parental or societal demands, and is evident in outdoor environments. Watch the crowds on a beach and you will see children, adolescents and adults all playing on, in or with the sand and water. For children, the beach is full of creative and physical opportunities from digging and building to creating dams and rivers, and splashing, stamping and rolling in both sand and water. Adolescents play team sports, bury each other and build complex tunnels and structures. Adults, often in the guise of playing with the children, will join in all these activities and even the most restrained of adults can be seen gently sifting sand and letting it fall through their fingers. The beach offers a myriad of other sensory experiences: the smell of food, the noise of nearby arcades and fair rides, the sound of the waves and of passing traffic. Other natural landscapes lend themselves to an equally wide range of sensory experiences and physical and creative activities, even urban ones. In the new shopping development near to where I live is a water feature comprising some 40–50 individual 'fountains' on a flat concrete bed. The jets of water follow a pattern and so are predictable but only if you stand and study them through a number of cycles. Without this, you can be caught unawares! All those who succumb to its magnetic pull also follow a pattern of activity, no matter what their age. They are tentative at first, watching and perhaps letting the water flow over their hand. Then they might move through a line of jets, carefully avoiding getting wet. Next, they 'accidently' get feet, legs or arms wet. They may dash across, jumping over the low jets or weave in and out of the high jets, gradually getting wetter and wetter. Finally, they hurl themselves with abandon into the jets, running, splashing and shrieking in delight. Just as with the therapists on the training day, once the barriers to playfulness are lowered, the adults soon tumble altogether. One boy of around six I watched got great delight and no doubt enormous sensory pleasure out of standing astride a jet and letting the water shoot up inside the legs of his shorts!

It is through our senses – sight, sound, touch, taste and smell – that we experience a connection between ourselves and the world around us. Liepmann (1974 in Oaklander 1988) suggests that even movement, the feeling of our muscles, joints and tendons in action, should be considered as an internalised touch sensation. However, at some point, our senses appear to become blurred and hazy, so that we operate primarily through our cognition, our thinking head. The increase in screen-based activities across our society underlines this and has ensured that many people of all ages spend much of their time in indoor environments despite the portable nature of many of these devices (see Chapter 2). Opportunities for physical activities and playful interactions would appear to have been significantly reduced. Much of what happens within our society is managed or constructed by adults, even when it is designed for young people. Leisure experiences are becoming more and more dependent on carefully designed, physically safe and costly artificial environments where rather than a rich 'natural' sensory experience, there is a complete sensory onslaught and overload of constructed sounds, sights and smells. Physical activities may be so safe as to be devoid of any challenge, or seen as so risky that the challenge has to be micro-managed in order to avoid any possibility of accidental injury.

As play therapists, we are rightly encouraged to undertake continuing professional development (CPD) activities and these often take the form of 'cognitive' activities: lectures, workshops, seminars or additional focused training. But we also need to attend to our body self and foster our inner playfulness, our creativity and our sense of connectedness to and interconnectedness with natural spaces. The simple outdoor activities that many of us already engage in such as gardening and walking have been shown to improve both our physical health and our emotional well-being (see Chapter 2). Our intimate relationships provide us with a safe space to explore our playfulness, sensuality and physicality. Activities using our voice and body can help us to overcome deep-rooted feelings of shame and embarrassment at 'making a fool of ourselves' or putting ourselves 'out there'. Working with art materials can increase our connection to our body self through the sensory feedback it provides. We must make the time to attend to ourselves if we are to attend to all those in our lives with whom we connect, particularly our clients.

The growth of interest in utilising our natural environment, the increase in the number of community choirs and singing groups and the growing variety of community-based dance classes from traditional ballet and tap to salsa, Le roc and Biodanza are all testament to a growing desire across society to reconnect with our body selves and our environment, establish and strengthen community connections, and nourish and replenish our energies.

Ensuring our personal resilience is crucial if we are to help our clients through the emotional upheaval that is the process of therapy.

The safe space

In discussing what it is that makes a space safe I suggest there are three areas to consider: physical safety, emotional containment and confidentiality. In proposing this, I do not see them as separate entities but as three interconnected elements which combined together create a feeling of safety and security for the client and the therapist, and, as has already been discussed earlier in this chapter, the safety of both should not be confused with control of the space by the therapist for their own reasons. We might consider that physical safety relates to the 'hard' structural aspects of the space and to the unintentional harm that might come to either the client or the therapist through physical activity or misuse of the toys and resources. Paying attention to the state of the fixtures and fittings and ensuring that there are no unprotected sharp corners and edges, loose flooring or unsafe furniture, that fire exits are not blocked and that there is appropriate ventilation and heating are common sense. Ensuring that you have considered what limitations there might need to be on physical contact and activities and being clear about these with the child when the need arises are basic good practice.

If we choose to offer an outdoor space, these two aspects of practice will still apply. The therapist is best prepared for the unexpected by assessing the suitability of any outdoor space prior to moving into it with the child, bearing in mind that to eliminate all risk is counter-productive. As we have discussed, risk taking and challenge are essential components in play if we are to facilitate growth and allow for transformation. Berger and Lahad (2013), in discussing their structured nature therapy and expressive arts programme 'A Safe Place', note that giving space to children for exploration and experimentation does not mean in itself that safety is compromised – it needs to be an ongoing guiding principle. However, any potential for harm needs to be considered alongside the benefit of activities so that we do not become so focused on potential risk that we over-protect children so that they become completely 'risk naïve' (Hackett 2008).

If work takes place in the playroom initially, the therapeutic alliance is established as described earlier, and since the outdoor space is offered as an extension to indoor space, it becomes another area to utilise for play which encompasses all three elements of EPR and into which the other resources can be taken. Any limits used within the indoor space apply outside and, if necessary, the use of the resources is re-negotiated with the child. Berger and Lahad (2013) note that if there is likely to be a challenge to limits from children who create boundary-testing situations, this will normally occur in the first sessions when working outside, just as it tends to happen within the playroom. My personal experience has been that because we have already established a relationship and limits have been clarified, the transition itself has not thrown up any difficulties. What may occur, however, is the need to establish additional limits to cope with a new situation that arises as a result of working outside. If we remain reflexive and attuned to our own feelings, we can identify if the need for the additional limits arises as a response to our own 'control' needs or because our client will otherwise be endangered.

Feeing physically safe is an integral part of feeling emotionally contained. In Jennings's circles of containment, care and attachment (2011), she suggests that containment is established pre-birth, with the mother's womb providing a 'circle full of safe water'. After the birth, the mother's arms continue to act as a physical container, while her attuned response creates emotional containment. Within the playroom, the therapeutic alliance is reminiscent of the attuned mother figure, and the therapist's acceptance, non-judgemental reflections, logical limits, openness and authenticity provide the emotional container. In this way, when moving out of the playroom, the child is contained by the symbolic walls of the alliance. Once outside, the 'nature mother' provides a container for both the therapeutic alliance and the therapeutic process so that the child can develop an interpersonal relationship with nature that will be sustained into the future. The space between the symbolic walls of the therapeutic alliance and the container of the 'nature mother' becomes a second intermediate playground, one which reflects the fluid and dynamic nature of the process of play therapy through its own transformations as weather and seasons change.

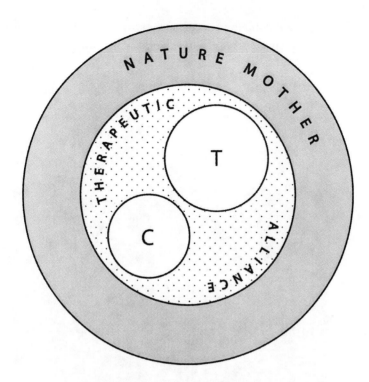

*Figure 4.1 The second intermediate playground –
containment by the 'nature mother'*

In using an outdoor space, not only do we need to consider its physical suitability, we also need to be aware of the personal meaning it may have for the child so that we can be alert to any potential issues that might be triggered. Jack (2010) notes that place attachment is an interaction between a person and an environment and is part of our overall identity. We give different places personal, social and cultural meanings which then become a framework for the construction of personal identity. Berger and Lahad (2013) tell us that spaces have both symbolic and archetypal meaning connected to a client's inner narrative, with different forms of spaces having different meanings and images for each client. A child who is afraid of the dark may dislike dense woods or forests but run freely across an open field or sandy beach. In contrast, a child who has never felt contained or safe within their familial relationships, who has no sense of body self, may prefer to use a smaller and more contained space such as an area with hedges, an open-sided tent or a purpose-built natural withy structure.

Figure 4.2 A contained outdoor space

When working within the playroom, emotional containment is supported by the predictability of the availability of the space, the length of the session, and routines that anchor the therapy in the present reality. However, moving into an outdoor environment does not mean abandoning these routines and structures. Before considering the use of an outdoor space, the therapist needs to ensure that access will be unrestricted. How the presence of other people will be managed needs to be considered with the child as far as possible before embarking on outdoor sessions. Since the majority of those clients I have worked with in school settings have been open about their sessions, the presence of other children has not in itself been problematic and we will discuss issues relating to confidentiality of the content of the sessions later in this chapter. Provided the space used is close to the playroom, the session length remains constant and any routines such as snacks and drinks can be maintained. (In the following chapter, I discuss the use of different outdoor spaces with three children in more detail, two of which were within school grounds, just beyond the playroom where the sessions took place. For the third client, public spaces were used, both close to the house and a car journey away.)

Jordan and Marshall (2010), in discussing counselling and psychotherapy in the outdoors, consider the use of the Lang's therapeutic 'frame' in connection with providing feelings of safety and containment and supporting the therapeutic process. They note that it sets the ground rules for the space and the manner in which the therapy is conducted, taking into account things such as roles, language, time, payment and physical space which need to be controlled to prevent transgressions between the therapist and the client. They suggest that although this provides for a very safe and stable space, in itself it might also limit the very nature of the therapeutic environment. Lang's view of the safe space was a sound-proofed room in a private office, within a professional building with absolute confidentiality and fixed positions for the therapist and client within the session. This alone might suggest so many physical boundaries that the therapy appears to be like a box within a box within a box, so that it is distinctly disconnected from reality or the client's life. The room itself was devoid of any extraneous decoration or personal items and there was no physical contact of any sort, not even a handshake. In this way, any issue that arose within the therapy was deemed to arise from the client rather than the 'frame' itself. However, Jordan and Marshall further note that developments in psychology, psychotherapy and eco-psychotherapy have all advocated the use of non-traditional settings, such as client's homes, community settings and natural spaces, so that such a precisely described 'frame' would appear to be far too restrictive. Within their own work in the outdoors with adults, they discuss confidentiality of the content of a session and the idea of a more fluid, contracting process, suggesting that they 'consider that fluidity within the contracting process involving a careful attention to emerging experience and the demands of the

outdoor setting is an absolutely central requirement for this work,'
in terms of providing protection for both client and therapist.'
Furthermore, they propose that working in outdoor environments
requires 'a "living frame", a movable and more dynamic encounter
which includes relationality with the living world around us in
the form of nature, the wind, rain, sunshine, a myriad of plant
and animal life, as well as the potentiality of encountering other
humans' (p.357).

Confidentiality is a complex and contentious issue when we
consider working in outdoor environments. The importance of it in
enabling clients to feel safe enough to give voice to complex and
difficult experiences should not be underestimated, but if we are
working with children and young people there are some specific
issues we need to consider both in relation to confidentiality in
general and within the outdoors in particular. Referrals for play
therapy come from a wide range of adults, including parents,
teachers, health and social care workers and voluntary agencies and,
very occasionally, a young person themselves. The decision that
play therapy is needed is therefore rarely the child's, and consent
from those with legal responsibility for the child is necessary for
the work to proceed. The Children Act of 1989 encourages the
participation of children and young people in decision making and
notes that the child's wishes should be ascertained in line with
their age and understanding. Since the Act defines a child as aged
0–18 years, until that age, in theory the young person remains the
responsibility of their parents. However, there is also a recognition
that as a young person becomes autonomous, although parental
responsibility should be exercised in the child's best interest, where
the child is of sufficient mental capacity to be able to understand
all the issues relating to the decision that needs to be made, they
have the right to make the decision for themselves. So embedded
within The Children Act is the concept of 'competence' resulting
from the Gillick case of 1986. This notion of competency and
sufficient mental capacity takes into account intelligence, maturity
and powers of reasoning (Fionda 2009). Additionally, there are the
ethical guidelines or codes of conduct by which therapeutic practice
is guided. Broadly speaking, these encompass six principles which
Daniels and Jenkins (2010) suggest come from the work of Daniluk

and Haverkamp and Thompson and which incorporate those of the British Association for Counselling and Psychotherapy (BACP). They are also the principles for ethical practice of the British Association of Play Therapists (BAPT):

- autonomy: the promotion of the client's freedom of choice and action

- fidelity: faithfulness, loyalty and the keeping of trust

- justice: achieving equality, fairness and avoiding discrimination

- beneficence: doing good and promoting the client's welfare

- non-maleficence: avoiding harm or damage to the client

- self-interest: promoting the self-knowledge, self-protection and self-development of the therapist.

Daniels and Jenkins further note that in recent years, a rights-based approach that aligns articles from the 1989 UN Convention on the Rights of the Child with these ethical principles is gaining ground and recognises that as children develop and become more competent, there is a reduction in the need for adult direction.

The challenge for play therapists is how to take into account guiding ethical principles and the child's rights within the context of a wide range of settings, including the outdoors. Often, decisions that must be made involve more than one ethical principle and in considering one, another may be open to being compromised. The BACP *Framework for Good Practice in Counselling and Psychotherapy* recognises that working with young people requires specific ethical awareness and competence:

> The practitioner is required to consider and assess the balance between young people's dependence on adults and carers and their progressive development towards acting independently. Working with children and young people requires careful consideration of issues concerning their capacity to give consent to receiving any service independently of someone with parental responsibilities and the management of confidences disclosed by clients. (BACP 2013, p.5)

For the purposes of this discussion, I am considering confidentiality issues prior to the age of 12 and in doing so recognise that any cut-off point is arbitrary since it is not chronological age that needs to be taken account of but the developmental stage of the child concerned. However, with those young people whose development follows a more typical pathway, competency to make informed and autonomous decisions is beginning to develop, and seeking their informed consent to access therapy becomes much more realistic. (For a fuller consideration of the issue of rights within therapy I suggest Wilson (2004), Alderson (2008), Daniels and Jenkins (2010) and Jones and Walker (2011)).

Daniels and Jenkins (2010), in considering the confidential space, note that within both wider society and within the therapeutic relationship, children can lack power, and that within therapy we can counteract this by offering a secure framework which maintains confidentiality and so empowers the child and upholds their potential for self-determination.

However, while we must always consider decisions with the best interests of the child in mind, respecting their autonomy and exploring any intentions implicit within our decision through supervision, we also need to avoid becoming so anxious about decisions we make that this impacts on both our confidence in our ethical and therapist self and our ability to be fully present for our client.

> No statement of ethics can totally alleviate the difficulty of making professional judgements in circumstances that may be constantly changing and full of uncertainties. By accepting this statement of ethics…(therapists are) committing themselves to engaging with the challenge of striving to be ethical, even when doing so involves making difficult decisions or acting courageously. (BACP 2013, p.3)

If those of us who include outdoor spaces in our practice do so because we have given full consideration to the ethical dilemmas this might pose, have used the supervision process to ensure that what we are doing remains in the best interest of our clients and their developing autonomy and we do so in good faith, this would seem to be both an ethical and professional stance. By adopting a more flexible and living framework that takes account of the need for confidentiality but does not tie us to the playroom we enable our clients to work with us to find creative solutions to problems we might encounter and this would seem to be empowering for both the client and the therapist.

In relation to disclosures of confidential materials, BAPT's *An Ethical Basis for Good Practice in Play Therapy* (2008) lists key ethical principles in line with those outlined earlier in this chapter. Under the principle of fidelity, it tells us that:

> Play Therapists establish relationships of trust with those with whom they work. Play Therapists honour and act in accordance with the trust placed in them. This principle obliges Play Therapists to maintain confidentiality and restrict disclosures of confidential information to a standard appropriate to their workplace and legal requirements. (p.4)

However, it also recognises that play therapy clients are generally non-autonomous and dependent on others to ensure their safety and well-being. So in terms of the content of sessions, a good rule of thumb would appear to be that aspects of the child's process through therapy may be discussed, with the child's agreement, with parents and relevant professionals who are in a position to support the child, but the content of the play remains confidential to the client and therapist unless there are safeguarding or legal reasons for disclosure. In saying this, I recognise that even agreeing that parents and professionals may be privy to aspects of the process will be contentious, but children do not exist in isolation. They live with parents and carers, they attend schools and have teachers and they may be involved with a number of other professionals whose role is to support their development and well-being. Perhaps we need to view this process of communicating as systemic working in order to see it as less problematic. In discussing systemic practice, Burnham (1998, p.xv) describes the importance of systemic rapport: 'the ability as a therapist to connect with one person in a relationship system while maintaining (a) the possibility of connecting with other persons and (b) the ability of those people to connect with each other'. This appears to offer a more positive frame of reference for involving other professionals where the therapist creates wider connections that can be of benefit to the child. The process of communicating information is not merely one way from therapist to parents or professionals. Each person who has a relationship with the child will have a perspective to contribute to the overall picture of that child. What we all need to be clear about is that we each have a specific role and that the boundaries and remit of each are clear and maintained. If we do not see other professionals as trustworthy, we need to take this to supervision to be clear that it is based on the reality of our contact with them and not on issues from our own lives that have not been fully processed. In relation to the play therapy sessions, the therapist should be clear about what information will shared and with whom and why before the therapy commences and this should be clearly put to the child and communicated to them in ways that are appropriate to both their developmental age and their communication style, the latter being particularly relevant for those children who have complex communication and learning needs. Maintaining confidentiality of content should be our guiding principle; however, BAPT's ethical guidelines do recognise that there may be valid reasons for a therapist to disclose information without consent, stating these to be to:

- refer to needed professional services

- obtain appropriate professional advice

- protect the client, play therapist or others from harm.

When involving children in decision making, in order to ensure that we act with due regard to their autonomy, we need to treat each client as an individual and explore their capacity to make decisions in relation to the individual situation about which the decision needs to be made. In doing this, we will need to take into account their life experiences, their stage of cognitive and emotional development and their individual personality rather than their chronological age (Daniels and Jenkins 2010).

In relation to working outdoors, we have already discussed the need to consider in advance and with the child how we will manage other people in the space. My work with parents and children together is focused on building a secure attachment and although initially I may have a small number of sessions with the child alone, sessions are conducted with either one or both parents present. The use of the outdoor space is crucial for the child to develop new embodied meaning and so develop a secure sense of body self to support the attachment process. For this work I have used public spaces and other people have witnessed our activities. However, I would suggest that they were completely unaware of the fact that this was a 'therapy' session and instead perceived us to be a family group enjoying our time together. The content of the sessions has personal meaning for the child and the child and parent together but to other people, it appears merely as play. They may make a judgement about the quality of it, but in my experience they rarely make a direct comment. If this should occur, it can be repelled playfully, as suggested in the earlier discussion about provocations. The meaning remains personal to the child and the parent and we have time away from the public space in which to process the session and the issues arising from it. (This will be discussed in more detail in the following chapter.)

A word about physical contact

Appropriate physical contact between human beings is necessary to healthy development, fulfilling relationships and intimacy, and non-verbal body language accounts for around 75 per cent of our communication. As we discussed in Chapter 2, too many images of the body, and in particular girls' and women's bodies, have become sexualised. So concerned are we as a society about the harm that might come to our children from paedophiles and strangers that perfectly ordinary and compassionate people refrain from helping a lost or hurt child because of how their actions might be perceived. In some nurseries, male staff are not allowed to change baby girls and no staff involved in the personal care of small children can attend to them unless they can be seen by other adults. While we must of course always be vigilant, the message we are sending our children and young people is that bodies are sexual in nature, and because of this, they are constantly at risk from adults. But our bodies are both part of us and that which holds all of us and we should be able to enjoy the fullest experience of them, both independently and in relation to the others around us. The general advice given to play therapists in training seems to be to not let a child sit on your lap, hug, cuddle or make bodily contact with you. In general, this is wise guidance since we are not in the role of the mother figure and would not want to confuse or mislead the child in relation to socially acceptable physical contact, particularly where a child's body or physicality has in some way been abused or their bodily integrity threatened.

However, as has been discussed, since our sense of body self plays such a crucial role in our ability to form and maintain mutually satisfying relationships, to repel physical contact per se is to tell the child that there is something wrong with their body, that it is an unacceptable part of them at a time when we are working to support them to become integrated. Instead of regarding touch in therapy as taboo, we are better placed if we reflect on why the need has occurred for whichever of us would be the initiator. If the child wants to hug us and we want to repel this, are we doing so because it is right for the child, or right for us? If we feel the need to cuddle the child, why is this? Does it tell us something about what the child themself needs or does it reflect our own experiences of wanting to be held? We need to feel that we are empowered to make decisions about the appropriateness of touch in relation to the context in which the need or desire is expressed and where we are unclear of its purpose use supervision to explore the issue further. Working in an outdoor environment offers many opportunities for appropriate and supporting touch if it is wanted by the child. The mutuality of helping one another to navigate a slippery slope or climb on to or around a natural barrier can be empowering for the child, since the therapist is not in a unique position of power as the one who can do the helping for one who needs help. Working together and using our bodies to negotiate physical challenges is much more reflective of the real world than remaining in the closed playroom where touch is unwanted and unwelcome.

PART II

Applications to Practice

Let Them Out

Walls, walls, walls closing in on me, please open the door
See this roof, shelter over me; well I don't want this shelter any
    more
And I want to feel the earth beneath my feet instead of this floor
Let me out and let me breathe in the open sky, high, high, high
Let me out and let me breathe in the open sky

For they must walk in the sunshine, dance in the rain
They must run with the wind, they need to do these things again
    and again
And look to their horizons and see their spirits fly
I believe they should breathe in the open sky, high, high, high
I believe I should breathe in the open
I believe we should breathe in the open
I believe they should breathe in the open sky
Let them out!

Beckers (2005) From the song arranged and
performed by Slipstream, Sophy Burleigh, Penny
Dunscombe, Bryony Penman and Sue Beckers

Chapter 5

Stepping Out

In this section I will consider three case studies: Samantha (Sammy), a child with profound and multiple learning (PML) needs, Peter, an adopted child, and Michael, a boy with complex social, emotional and behavioural (SEB) needs.

Although the play detailed is real, the names of the children are not, and some sessions have been integrated for focused illustration but remain true to each child's progress through the play therapy. In each of these cases, the nature of my role in the play was unique to the context of the therapy and to my own style of working, which is undoubtedly eclectic in its theoretical perspective. I have not drawn from different sources at random, but the experience of working with children who have often been described as 'hard to reach' has required me to walk my own path. In doing so I have discovered that sometimes we have to take a deep breath and plunge into uncharted waters with the belief that our clients will show us what it is they need. For all of us, having someone present to witness our experiences, to validate them and work with us to find a place where we can gain new meaning for ourselves, will be one of the most transformational experiences we can have.

In making an analysis of my work in the outdoors, I have used a simple structure which starts with the playroom sessions and '*settling*' where the therapeutic alliance is created, progresses through '*transition*', the move to the outdoors, and concludes with '*transformation*', the changes that occur.

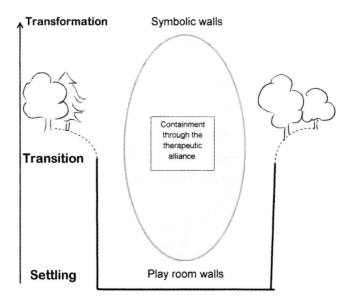

Figure 5.1 The three stages of the process

CASE STUDY 1: SAMMY

Trapped in their bodies, too many children are born this way
Bound, constrained, frustrated, is it accident or is it fate?
They've so much to do, so much to say
Who said that life had to be this way?
Let them out and let them breathe in the open sky, high, high, high
Let them out and let them breathe in the open sky.

> Beckers (2005) From the song arranged and
> performed by Slipstream, Sophy Burleigh, Penny
> Dunscombe, Bryony Penman and Sue Beckers

We first met Sammy in Chapter 4 in a session at Forest School. She has grey matter heterotopia with associated severe epilepsy and profound developmental delay. Grey matter heterotopia is a malformation of the cortex or surface of the brain so that clumps of grey matter, normally on the surface of the brain, are in the wrong place, trapped deep within it. Grey matter contains nerve cells critical to the processing of information involved in muscle control and to sensory perception. Sammy needed stimulation to ensure she did not exist only in her own world, and linear movement such as swinging to provide vestibular stimulation which her sensory system required. She needed to develop both her core stability and a sense of body self, described in an occupational therapy report as information from muscles and joints communicating the position of her body in space to the brain. The report also noted that her sensory processing difficulties caused inappropriate reaction to touch, but that deep pressure and calming activities would help to organise her nervous system and support effective sensory processing. Sammy was seven when she was referred for play therapy and was attending a specialist local authority school for children with profound and multiple learning (PML) needs. The objective of the therapy was to support the development of her communication, social interaction and play.

Within the school I had a playroom in a building close to the main school in which I had created a safe nurture corner with a large bean bag, soft blankets and pillows and cushions, and I had used different corners in the room to reflect the EPR paradigm. In addition to the safe space, there was a sand tray, a water tray and small world toys, a well-protected area for messy play and art work, an area for the musical instruments and other sensory toys, a role-play area with puppets and lengths of fabrics, and a table if needed. There was also a large round 'gathering' drum. I had been made aware that Sammy 'ate' everything she came into contact with and tended to move around in an uncontrolled way and so I exchanged the sand and water trays for some small pots of sensory foodstuffs: cornflakes, small cereal hoops and raisins. I was intending to use an Intensive Interaction approach in our session together.

Intensive Interaction is a way of creating 'communication moments' by responding playfully to the child's actions through sensitive imitation, mirroring and joining in using voice and body language and running commentary. The teacher (or therapist) makes a space for the child to lead the activity, and the content and flow are developed by their responses (Hewitt 2009). In essence it uses a process very similar to non-directive play therapy and is used to develop communication in children with PML needs. However, before I started the sessions in the playroom, I wanted to see Sammy in a familiar environment so I spent time with her in the outdoor area attached to her classroom. Due to the severe epileptic fits Sammy sometimes had, staff were concerned about her being on her own with me initially. Although generally I would include any additional attending adults in the play, in this instance, because establishing a relationship with Sammy would require me to be focused fully on her, I agreed that one of the teaching assistants from her class could attend the session in an 'observer' role only. Although we met weekly during term times, there were long gaps during the holidays and once a month she missed her session to go on a visit to an animal sanctuary with her class.

When I first saw Sammy, she was lying on the ground outside in a corner of the play area, picking up leaves and small sticks and putting them in her mouth. She appeared oblivious to what was happening around her, lost in her own world and unaware my presence. She scratched through the leaves making little noises but made no response to my attempts to mirror her movements or echo her voice. During our early sessions together, she pounced on the pots of food and frantically stuffed the contents into her mouth, spilling much on the floor and then scrabbling around to finish up every last scrap. She usually brought some bells with her from the classroom and often an old catalogue or some sheets of paper which were her transitional objects. She carried these things about the room, gathering up additional items and scuffing one foot along in a plastic bowl. Every so often, she would clamber up onto the gathering drum and walk over it. She disliked any physical contact, but would sit on her heels and bounce hard on the ground or rock frantically on a chair. It had been explained to me that in order to feel 'balanced', such as we might when we are still, Sammy needed movement.

As well as the physical and mental impairments Sammy had, through supervision I reflected on what it must be like for those parents whose baby does not respond in the usual way and the impact this would have on both establishing a connection and providing containment through holding, feeding, rocking and soothing the infant. Not only would her impairments have hindered the development of her body self, but the responses they would have induced would have made it very difficult for her mother to have provided care and containment in a way that might have given her a sense of body self.

Settling

Due to Sammy's profound developmental delay and cognitive impairment, forming a connection with her from which we could establish a therapeutic alliance needed both time and patience. Developing the usual rituals and routines that would have been created together, such as removing our shoes and putting them by the door, hanging up coats and welcoming each other, was problematic, so other opportunities needed to be found. There were two songs that Sammy liked – 'Row, Row, Row, your Boat' and 'Rock-A-Bye-Baby' – which I sang repeatedly throughout our early sessions, along with a naming song I had made up. When I sang the first song, we developed a game where I held her by the forearms and gently rocked her to and fro, providing the linear movement her vestibular system needed and also helping to increase her awareness of her body. With feet braced on the floor, she showed she was beginning to develop increased core stability. After around four sessions, she would hold out her hands as if in invitation to me to play the game. Communication had been established. In order to create a more calming ritual, I would sit on the floor in the soft corner and sing 'Rock-A-Bye-Baby'.

For several weeks she did not really connect with this except occasionally to lie on the bean bag for a moment or two. Thinking about her developmental delay, and early 'hide away' games, I covered her with a soft blanket on one occasion but she tossed it away and ran off. I repeated this each time she lay on the beanbag and sometimes she remained there long enough for me to play a brief game of 'peepo', pulling the blanket down and then over her again. Gradually she began to spend longer in the beanbag and to lie quietly for a few moments. I started to pat her gently on the back in a rhythm approximating a heartbeat. Somehow she could tolerate this. She stayed there a little longer as the weeks progressed and at one point climbed onto my lap and snuggled very closely. Until this point, our physical contact had been 'shared' through the rocking game. This represented Sherbourne's second stage and in order to return to the earliest developmental stage and resume a more typical trajectory, Sammy needed to go back to the caring 'with' developmental movement activities.

Being on my lap, wrapped in a blanket, was appropriate, particularly since because of her emotional and cognitive impairment, she needed a lengthy concrete experience of being physically held before any sense of emotional containment could occur. So we had established a connection through non-verbal communication and song and she was able to experience physical containment. Our therapeutic alliance was established. During this time her teaching and care staff noted that when she was on someone's lap, she tried to get so close, it was as if she was trying to climb inside you! Symbolic of her rebirth perhaps?

Transition

During the first six months of the therapy, as Sammy's trust in me developed, the therapeutic alliance was strengthened. The level of playfulness between us increased, I felt she had developed an attachment to the playroom and a discernible structure began to emerge. The accompanying adult and I would walk Sammy to the room where she would explore all the resources, often throwing them onto the floor. This was difficult for the teaching assistant in the room because they still held some association between this and 'naughtiness'. Sometimes they went to pick the items up and I needed to reassure them that it was fine to leave things where they had fallen and to respond to such acts in a very different way. She would eat all of the food in the pots as fast as she could. After around ten minutes of gathering things into her bowl, Sammy would retreat to the corner and play with her back to me while I sang the naming song and rhythmically patted her back. Eventually she would be ready for more interactive play. At the end of the session, I sang a 'goodbye' song and we returned with her to the classroom. She was beginning to respond to her name and on occasions would make eye contact with me, holding my gaze fleetingly and sometimes making her vocalisations in response to my echoing. The head of the school worked with the staff to develop a more individual curriculum for Sammy based on physical and sensory activity since observation of the play therapy session was enabling staff to develop a different approach in the classroom and was giving them confidence to try new approaches.

At around this time, Sammy's parents were experiencing relationship difficulties and she and her mother moved from the family home to live with a relative. As a result, she became more distressed during the sessions. Occasionally, she would not leave the classroom and I had to work with her in the small adjoining sensory room. Although she had developed a place attachment with the playroom, she needed the safety of the classroom, her 'secure base' when things got stressful. In either space, her distress was palpable; she would bounce hard onto the floor, over and over again, wailing and crying, her face contorted. In the playroom, she would push everything onto the floor or hug me suddenly, climb into my lap, cuddle me and then rush off around the room. Mirroring her movements and her voice, and through parallel processing, I picked up her distress in my upper chest area, accompanied by a strong need to 'break out'. Despite the impairments she had, she was clearly processing the anger, distress and frustration she was experiencing and these were deeply embodied experiences. I felt that this reflected an unconscious need in Sammy to break free from her own internal world and connect to the outer world, which always seemed to be just beyond her grasp. The playroom, even with all its sensory toys and resources, felt closed and static, much as I imagined Sammy's inner world to be. Some 'real', external experience was needed to match the process she was going through.

We continued like this for two more months, during which time new play equipment was installed in the playground, including a 'bird's nest' swing (see cover picture). Our sessions remained characterised by Sammy's movement from her corner to my lap to the space in the room and then back to the corner. Sometimes it felt as if the room was becoming too small and she was like a small caged animal, following a continuous track around the room in an effort to gain both emotional and physical release. Several weeks later, staff felt there was no longer a need for them to join us, since she had been free of fits in school for some time and so she came to the session with me alone. She and her mother had also returned to the family home, although her father was no longer there. She appeared much less distressed and her play was more focused. On several occasions, she didn't stuff the food into her mouth but picked it up and scrunched it in her hands, getting real sensory pleasure from the action. When I offered objects to her to include in her bowl, she would select some to add whereas previously she had rejected them all immediately. During one session she climbed onto the drum and then jumped into my arms. I slowly let her drop away from me until she was upside down, secure in my arms but looking at the world in a new way, which immediately brought a smile to her face. She had a much stronger sense of her body self, was able to trust it to me and was exploring a new way of being in it and with it. She was gradually creating new embodied meaning.

During the next session she started to take my hand and pull me towards the door and on the way back to the classroom she ran off across the playground to the bird's nest swing. Her classroom staff had been using this to provide the stimulation for her sensory system and she loved it! For the next two sessions, it became increasingly difficult to get her into the playroom as whenever she went out of the building, she headed for the swing. Once inside the room, she spent a lot of the time in her distressed position, bouncing on her heels. Through signing, I tried telling her we could go there after we had spent some time inside, but she was set on the swing. My supervisor asked me why I didn't follow the lead she was giving me and I realised it was because I was unsure how I was going to be able to control the situation if I did. What if she fell and hurt herself running to the swing? What if we got out there and I couldn't get her back in? I had fallen into thinking she was vulnerable because of her medical issues, when everything she was doing demonstrated a strong inner core. These were my issues, not Sammy's. I needed to trust the process.

A new routine needed to be established between us. I knew Sammy liked going to the animal sanctuary and liked the horses there. I sourced a large lycra pilates band which I doubled high around her waist, holding it at the back like a pair of riding reins. I made up a rhyme to sing about a little pony and encouraged her to trot beside me as if we were a pair of horses. Because the band was elastic, it gave her something to pull against, giving her an experience of her body's possibility for strength. Sometimes she would fall to the ground and I would try playfully to pull her up with the band so that she bounced as if she was in a purpose-built baby bouncer. Within the playroom we had moved through Sherbourne's 'with' and 'shared' phases and this gave her an experience of resistance, of using her body in an 'against' action. In this way we also made safe progress to the swing. I had lined the basket with a big blanket, and she brought her beloved bells and tattered catalogue, her transitional objects. For several weeks I pushed her on the swing, singing the songs we had used in the playroom to give some continuity through the transition to the outdoors.

Transformation

By the time we moved our session into the outdoor area, Sammy and I had been working together for around eight months. Working outside offered her some real sensory experiences that were impossible to set up in the playroom. Apart from the rocking motion she needed, there was the weather, the wind in the tress, the puddles and mud on the ground, the sound of birds and noises from the nearby streets. When the weather was cold or the rain light, we went to the swing, but if the rain was heavy, we worked in the small room attached to the classroom. If we returned to the playroom she became distressed, and I felt this was because she had processed a lot of difficult issues here earlier in the year and being there was too painful. To continue to develop Sammy's core strength, I put the pilates band around her back and under her arms so that I could hold it and face her. I used it to pull her gently and start the swing, and as it moved to and fro, she pushed against the band to increase the height. She was gaining a real sense of both her body itself and its capacities to cause movement, thus gaining an embodied experience of transformation. I brought a hoop to the swing and hooked it around her back and pulled her to fro with it from the front. She loved this, and would hold the sides of the hoop and pull hard to increase the arc of the movement. When I stopped pushing, she would reach out and pull my hand to communicate her desire to get going again. She loved to be pushed up high and would smile and chatter as the movement relaxed her. Sometimes she knelt in swing, testing her ability to balance, and often she would burrow into the blanket, rest her head against the side ropes and appear to be sleeping!

Since the motion of the swing provided the sensory stimulation she needed, her level of engagement with me increased quickly. When the swing slowed down, she reached for my hands, and I played 'pat-a-cake' with hers. She responded with her own hands and over time, we incorporated a 'high five', which one of her teaching assistants had taught her. She was now making good eye contact, focusing on whoever was working with her and holding the gaze for longer. One area that was still difficult was getting her back into the building, despite the use of the band! She was very quick and would often run off, sometimes onto other play equipment, but sometimes into the building towards the entrance hall where she would lie on the floor in front of the first set of exit doors. If she went on to other equipment I would walk towards the building, turn and sign 'finished' to let her know we needed to go in. If she didn't follow I would go back a few steps, repeat this, and then walk towards the building. It generally worked, but if I got as far as the exit doors, it didn't! Staff would come from the class to collect her. In discussion with the staff, we realised that this was because they often used the swing towards the end of the day just before she went home. On these occasions, she found it difficult to settle back in the classroom because she wanted to go home. Moving her session back to an earlier time and having a member of staff collect her from the playground set a new routine but worked well. After five or six sessions of being collected, she would follow me back to the main building and we gradually replaced this with the 'trotting horses', returning side by side, with me holding the reins.

There was a period of three weeks when things changed at home again and Sammy was very distressed, returning to bouncing and wailing. She seemed tired and listless and her grip on the hoop had no real strength, but after 10–15 minutes of swinging, she relaxed and even regained some energy. Our play had a consistent structure, and the predictability of this also relaxed her. It was familiar and she did not need to work at anything. However, I felt that some small challenge might help to develop her body awareness. One of the songs I had introduced her to was 'Speed Bonny Boat'. The rhythm of the song matched the rhythm of my pushes on the swing and I began to create narrative about going on an adventure across the sea. Our songs had a definite nautical flavour since I continued to use 'Row, Row' and added a revised version of 'What Shall We Do with a Drunken Sailor?' changing it to 'What Shall We Do in Stormy Sea?' As I sang this, I would gently rock the swing from left to right so that it wobbled. At first Sammy looked startled but soon she would kneel in the basket and hold my hands to indicate that I should wobble it. I began to wobble it a little harder while it was swinging gently and although at first she was unnerved, she laughed and I began to wobble it when the swing was going faster and higher. I tied some fine fabric to the ropes of the swing to create sails and these would waft across her face and over her head giving her additional sensory stimulation. Sometimes, she would kneel and catch the fabric, using it to pull herself to and fro. Then she started holding her hand up for a 'high five' while she was swinging, and when the swing slowed, she would hang over the front edge to watch her shadow or drag her fingers over the ground below. She still brought something with her from the classroom each time but more often than not these remained buried in the folds of the blanket. Her confidence in her strength and balance was clear and her core strength had improved significantly. She was engaged by what we were doing and interacting with me with playfulness. She was able to 'control' the activity by indicating what she wanted to do and had expressed a range of emotions from distress, anger and frustration to pleasure and joyfulness. This was a very different girl to the one I had encountered in the corner of the playground eating leaves!

Sammy's story – the voyage of adventure

We're off on an adventure! Over the sea we'll go. Climb aboard and hold on tight. Off we go. There's a gentle breeze a-blowing (swings starts) but I see clouds ahead. (swing goes higher). Uh Oh!, Here we go, here comes the storm (swing begins to wobble). Hold on tight, the storm is here (swing is going high with sudden wobbles and I sing 'What Shall We Do in a Stormy Sea?') Hold on tight until it's over! Oh look, the wind is stopping (swing begins to slow and fabric flutters down). The storm is passing, the sun is coming (swing slows right down). Ah yes, here comes the sun, our boat will rock gently on the waves (swing wobbles gently and I sing 'Speed Bonny Boat'). We're almost home, gently now and let's stop.

CASE STUDY 2: PETER

Peter was referred for play therapy when he was three-and-a-half as he was in a foster placement and due to be adopted for a second time, his previous adoptive placement having broken down. His early life had been chaotic, with episodes of violence from his father towards his mother. He had had several periods of foster care starting when he was three months old, although with the same carers. Since birth, he had made many attachments with adults who were no longer part of his life. The first time I met him I was touched by a heavy presence of sadness which accompanied him into the room. He seemed diminished and bowed down by the sheer weight of it.

Settling

The plan that was agreed was for me to work with Peter in the weeks prior to the adoption to develop a relationship with him, and then to work with him and his adoptive parents together to support the development of healthy attachments. Our first sessions took place in a clinic setting where we had a small room with a large wooden fort, a basket of play food, a doctor's kit and some puppets. I added a small tray of sand, bubbles, crayons and paper, a baby doll, a blanket and a bottle, various textured balls, some books and a jigsaw of a mother duck and ducklings. In addition to these resources, the room also had a small, low table and three chairs, a large square floor cushion and a small bench which the puppets sat on.

Peter arrived at the clinic in a taxi, accompanied by Hannah, the transport escort. Coming into the reception area for the first session, he was cheerful and smiling and chatted to the reception staff and he was happy to take my hand to see the fish at the far end of the reception area. In common with many children within the public care system, he had cultivated a 'likeable' exterior which was likely to be at odds with his inner 'unlikeable' self, and he made rapid attachments to adults who showed pleasure in his company. I had an electronic 'fob' on a frog key ring with which to open the door to the corridor where our room was located. Peter noticed this straightaway, wanting to hold it and naming it 'Froggie'. Once in the corridor, there were a number of plain grey doors on either side, distinguishable only by their position along the corridor and a small number high up below the peephole in them. We counted off the doors on the left to our room, number three. Once inside, Peter took off his coat and we put it on the chair in the corner and I took off my shoes and put them underneath the chair. I had brought a new pair of slipper socks for him to wear but although he allowed me to help him off with his shoes, he didn't want the slipper socks on. I asked him if we should play 'this little piggy' with his toes but he didn't want them touched and said he wanted his shoes back on. At this point, his demeanour changed from cheerful to sad and he sat on the floor with his head down, flopping at the waist as if there was no substance to his middle. Giving attention to any aspect of his body seemed problematic for him. I put the slipper socks on the chair and told him they were there if he wanted them and it would be okay if he didn't.

I asked him if he thought he could draw a picture of himself but he didn't want to draw. I had brought my resources in a big, deep, zipped bag which I had left in the corner of the room. He spotted this, unzipping it to explore its contents, almost falling into it head first! He found a large soft toy Mickey Mouse, which he pulled out excitedly and tossed onto the floor. He rummaged about a bit more and found some bubbles. I opened the pot to blow some but after trying to catch a few he lost interest, spotted the play food and told me he was 'starvin'. I reflected that he was starving, that he had an empty feeling in his tummy and needed to fill it. He explored the contents of the food basket and said he was going to make some dinner for himself and then some for me. He found pizza for himself and chose to prepare chicken, cheese, chips and a bun for me with a cup of tea.

His 'hunger' was to be a recurring theme, a reflection of the emptiness within; a lack of a full and rounded embodied self as a result of inconsistent attunement, affection and affirmation in his early years. There was also the strong possibility that at points during his life, food and the comfort it brings had been denied him. Without this early nurture characterised by caring and containing physical contact, our healthy body self will not be established and we may seek other ways to gain a sense of our body's existence. Orbach (2004, p.27) in discussing early neglectful experiences suggests that:

> This adapted, precarious body not only requires constant affirmation but is so lacking in continuity that its viability for the individual is in question…and depends upon creating and surviving emergencies…This surviving of or recovering from emergencies provides the individual with the sense that their body exists.

Peter filled the empty void of his body self with food. Perhaps paradoxically, there was also something there that might have reminded him of the only times he felt the closeness of an adult, on the occasions when he was fed. Following his making of the dinners, he wanted to go outside to see the corridor, perhaps in an attempt to escape those feelings the play had aroused. After this, he didn't really settle to anything else, he just kept putting out dinners for us, telling me he was starving and thirsty. Periodically, he flopped onto the floor cushion with a sigh and seemed almost to collapse in on himself. Finally, the small alarm clock rang to tell us we had ten minutes left before we had to tidy up. After we had put the toys away and collected his coat from the chair, we went into the kitchen next door for a drink.

We began to establish a routine for the beginning and end of the sessions. 'Froggie' unlocked the first door and then Peter tried to find the door to the playroom by counting initially and then simply by remembering its position. Inside, we dealt with his coat and my shoes since he still wanted to keep his shoes on. I tried to include some nurture play using small cotton balls to check to see if he had any 'hurts' that he needed me to attend to, but he still wanted no physical contact. Although he always came back to the food play, he did briefly use the other resources and during the second session, he started to throw the puppets and soft toys about the room, laughing and squealing as they hit the wall or fell onto the floor. In contrast to his body when he flopped onto the floor cushion, his movements were co-ordinated and strong, although his aim was not too accurate and he hit himself on the head with the toys on several occasions as he tried to throw them. This made us laugh all the harder. In this session, he seemed to be able to take pleasure in his body's movements, almost as if he had forgotten how good it can feel to move around spontaneously. In his first foster placement, he had limited play space and was often contained indoors, and his current foster carer presented as tense and at times agitated and I suspected his movements were quite heavily curtailed with her too. When he was busy, he forgot he was starving or thirsty. We finished with tidy-up time and a drink in the kitchen before putting on his coat and returning to the reception area to wait for Hannah.

At the start of session three, he saw the jigsaw of the mother duck and three ducklings on the table. He looked at it and after several moments, told me he didn't have a mummy but he was getting a new one. I reflected that he was getting a new mummy and wondered how that might feel but he had already gone to get the animals. Play centred around making dinner for us both and he continued to be hungry. On one occasion, he piled a huge amount of food on his plate and told me again that he was starving. I commented that he must have a big hole inside for all the food and that sometimes we can have sad feelings inside that make us feel empty. I wondered if there was anything he might need to draw, but he said 'No' and carried on with his food play, making me several cups of tea and watching to make sure I drank them.

When he arrived for the following session, he was buoyant despite having a cold. He told me he was thirsty and I reminded him that we got a drink after we tidied up at the end. He was not happy and looked very deflated, lying on the floor cushion with a sad expression on his face. He was not interested in any attention to his 'hurts', fiddled with the sand tray and drawing paper, but did not settle to anything. He told me again that he was thirsty and I noted that it's hard when you want something and you have to wait and he flopped again as his resilience waned. He moved in and out of this low mood, distracted from it for short periods by the bubbles and then he found the baby doll in my bag, wrapped it in a blanket and laid it carefully on the big cushion saying, 'The baby is crying because he wants a bottle'. He found the bottle, filled it with sand and gave the baby 'a drink' with it. We talked about babies, feeding and burping and he tried to drink from the bottle of sand. I considered his 'starvin' empty feeling and how he often flopped when he was sad. The sand, if he drank it, would be like ballast, something to weight him down, to make him more solid and permanent. It is as if by feeding the baby, he was feeding his body self, nurturing and attending to it as no one else did. I told him that the sand was not for drinking but I could bring some juice for the bottle for the next session and he liked this idea and said he was thirsty now! When the ten minute alarm sounded, he looked relieved and rushed to gather up the toys so he could go to the kitchen for a drink. Our parting ritual was to tidy up, have a drink in the kitchen, and then go back down the corridor where he stretched up on tiptoe to press the button to unlock the door to reception. Hannah was there to collect him and he turned as he went, saying goodbye and reminding me not to forget the juice!

We had been getting on well together, but I felt he was finding it hard to trust me with his still fragile self. He had had so many losses in his life – his birth parents, his first foster carers, his first adoptive parents whom he was with for over a year, nursery and care staff and now his current foster carers. I felt that the juice I promised would be very significant and had the potential to secure our relationship and allow the therapeutic alliance to fully develop.

When Peter arrived for his next session I was still in the playroom and he told the receptionist to 'go and get that person Ali!' When I appeared, he called my name loudly and ran across the reception area, putting out his arms as if to hug my legs and then stopped, unsure of what to do, not trusting me to accept him. He checked that I had remembered the juice and walked to the door, calling for 'Froggie' to come and unlock it. He found the playroom door quickly and once inside, asked about his juice. I showed him the bottle with juice in it, which the monkey puppet was looking after. He smiled and took a drink. During this and our remaining two sessions before he moved to live with his new adoptive parents, he processed much about his sadness, which he indicated he felt in his upper chest area (his heart?). When I asked him if it was a big sad or a small sad, he said, 'It's small'.

My own thoughts are that he was both the smallness and the 'sad', a small sad being, sad for himself, for all the losses he had had and for the unlovable boy he felt he was. He threw the 'naughty' animals around the room and told me they were sad because they had been naughty. He found some emotion cards with bears on them, picked out a big grumpy one and said, 'Daddy shouts – makes me sad', and told me, 'The bear is crying cos he's bin shouted at'. There was a heavy atmosphere in the room, and he found one more card of a small bear with his back to us. 'He's sad, he shouted at the Daddy and the Daddy shouted back'. His own face looked very sad and I got my special box in which I kept a small mirror, the cotton balls for helping 'hurts' and a small bottle of hand lotion. Before I could offer anything, he noticed a small cut on my hand and said 'You have a hurt hand' and dabbed at it with the cotton ball. I asked him if he had any hurts and he said he had had a 'jection' in his arm and allowed me to pat it gently with a cotton ball. Then I asked if he would like some lotion on his hand and he held out his palm for some which I gently rubbed it in. These two small actions were so significant. He could at last trust himself with me, knew he was acceptable with all his hurt and pain. He wanted to put some lotion on the back of my hand, rubbed it on carefully and the therapeutic alliance was firmly established.

Transition

In the last session before Peter moved to his new family, he was very subdued and sad. His foster mother had been cross with him for biting the younger child in the house and he found it very difficult to settle. He wanted more and more juice and made lots of dinners. His emotional resilience was depleted and the empty space inside him could not be filled. He drew two faces, his and mine, mine smiling, his with a downturned mouth. I had suggested to the social worker that when he went to his adoptive family, we should have a short break to allow them time together which would mean we would not meet for two weeks. Unfortunately, the adoption date had been brought forward by over a week and I had only found out the previous day.

I needed to tell Peter that we would not be seeing each other for a short time but that I would see him again with his new family. I had drawn up a chart of 'sleeps' to show how many days it would be and asked him if wanted to look after one of my soft toys, a leopard with a very sad expression on his face, until the next time I saw him. He found the bear cards again and picked out one happy bear and one sad bear. The happy bear wanted a new mummy, the sad bear didn't. We talked about how sometimes we do want to do something but because it can be scary, we can also not want to do it. Following this, the animals all got tossed around the room; many of them were sad and needed a drink of juice to cheer them up. Even some of the food got thrown about, as if nothing could be relied on any more and the resulting chaos seemed a reflection of both his short life to date and the mix of feelings he had about yet another move and whether he would be accepted or not.

My next session with Peter took place in his new home, just three days after he had moved in there. I heard him calling me while I was waiting for the front door to be opened. He was very excited and showed me his new bedroom, the bathroom, the sitting room and the garden and I felt he was already beginning to develop some attachment to it. He fetched the toy he had been looking after and showed me the 'sleeps' chart which was stuck on the fridge. Although I had suggested that both adoptive parents, Julia and David, spend the sessions with me and Peter, David's work schedule could not accommodate this and I would work with Julia and Peter to start with. Julia told me quietly that food remained a significant issue, even though she and David reassured him that he would always have plenty to eat in his new house. He had been tending to overeat and then developed stomach ache, creating and surviving the emergency which let him know his body still existed. I talked to Julia about opportunities to go outdoors, to re-establish his core physicality, his robust and resilient body self. She said that Peter has asked if we could go to the park and that they had been there once already but he had been reluctant to go on anything. We walked to the park across the street and up a hill. Peter took his scooter with him, pushing it all the way. Going up the hill he got tired but Julia encouraged him to keep going and he managed it. In the park, he wanted to go on the slide but was still reluctant to go up the steps. Julia encouraged him to have a go and I went to the bottom of the slide to catch him if he needed me to. He began to climb and with Julia's continuous encouragement he got to the top and sat for a while. I noted that he knew how to get up the steps and I was sure he would know how to come down the slide. I wondered aloud if it looked a bit scary from where he was and reminded him I would stay at the bottom. He hovered, but then was off, arriving at the bottom safely. Julia told him he was very brave and asked him if he wanted another go and saying she would take a photo to show David. With her encouragement he climbed the steps again and waited at the top until she was ready with her camera. He was smiling and looked pleased with himself! There were some round portholes on one part of the slide and we played 'peepo' as he went on it again, several times. After this, he rode his scooter around and dropped it next to another similar one before he ventured on a second, slightly higher slide. With the activity, he was gaining in confidence, getting a stronger sense of his physicality and strength and finding that his body could be a source of pleasure. There was a group of adults and children eating ice cream nearby and he suddenly appeared to feel sad and said he wanted to go home. Perhaps he had been reminded of other times when he had been part of a family group, was overwhelmed by the feeling and needed to escape.

We returned to the house and had a drink around the kitchen table. I told him I had ten more minutes before I had to go. He needed to go to the toilet but rolled about on the bottom stairs laughing. Julia came along and told him she was the Tickle Monster and he laughed, squirming as she caught him, enjoying the playfulness of the moment. I sensed that he was beginning to know that he had a real 'place' there even though it was early days. When he came down, I was packing my bag and he flopped onto the sofa with his back to me, not wanting me to leave! I told him that I knew it was hard when people needed to go before he wanted them to but that I would be back the following week. He eventually came to the door to say goodbye and was cheered by Julia who reminded him they had to take the dogs for a walk after lunch.

Transformation

The next week when I arrived, Julia told me that Peter had asked if we could go to Jungle Joe's, an indoor play park a short car ride away. She felt that he would probably only stay a short while as he was anxious about going and suggested that he had only gone on the slide the week before because I had been there. I told her that I thought he felt secure with her and was developing a real attachment to her. Jungle Joe's was a large, echoing barn-like place and there were a number of other children there, most of them younger than Peter but one or two older than him. There was a big netted ball pit, a soft play area and a very high slide which was in two sections with a small 'landing' halfway down.

Julia went to get some drinks and Peter decided to go into the ball pit first of all; in his excitement, he threw some balls around, narrowly missing another child. I gently told him that we needed to be careful and to make sure we didn't hurt anyone and he plunged back in to the balls but as he came up he threw some more. I reminded him that we needed to be careful but his head went down and he left the pit, moving right away from it. He was upset as he thought he had been naughty and that once again he was the 'unlovable' boy. I reflected that he thought he'd been naughty and he felt upset but we needed to keep each other safe and make sure we didn't hurt the other children. I told him I knew it was hard to carry on playing when you felt upset and I would wait by the ball pit until he was ready. He returned and disappeared into the back of the ball pit, reappearing on the steps to the top level. Julia had returned and we affirmed his bravery. He disappeared again and emerged on a high walkway to the slide. I caught Julia's eye and saw that although she was smiling at him, she was also very anxious. I called up to him, told him he knew such a lot about climbing high and gave him two 'thumbs up'. He disappeared again and came out at the top of the slide. He looked tiny perched high above us with a seemingly massive drop to the first landing. Suddenly he was off, sliding onto his side on the landing, and almost rolling to the next slide. He managed to get himself sitting half upright and was off again. Julia was at the bottom and I could almost see her heart pounding. Peter landed at the bottom in a heap, scrambled up and was hugged by Julia momentarily. He wriggled out, his face a mixture of elation and panic! His body was alive; it had survived the crisis and needed to recover from the emergency. He ran around the room almost as if he was being physically chased by his feelings, running fast to get away from them and then Julia finally scooped him into her arms and held him tight, telling him how brilliant he was. He slowly relaxed and when she let him go, the emergency was over and he had recovered with her help, and had had a new embodied experience, one of containment and security. We sat and had a drink together then Peter wanted to go on the slide again. This time he had a little more control and allowed Julia to catch him at the bottom. She was establishing herself as his safe base. He went on it several more times and each time, his confidence in his body grew as he developed new embodied meaning of himself as competent and capable. At one point he was on the high walkway which has a large soft ball above it on a zip wire so it can be swung from one end to the other. Peter was almost at the end when another boy sent the ball down and it bumped him, although not very hard. He managed to get back past the ball and tried to scramble down but Julia called to him, telling him he was okay, that he could stay there and try to get to the end again because the ball had stopped there. He focused on her and managed to calm himself, returning to the end of the walkway and going onto the slide again. I had to leave shortly after this but the following week Julia mentioned that they had stayed for some time, and Peter learned from another boy how to fire the ball cannon and they had then continued to play happily together.

When I arrived for the next session, Julia was ironing and Peter and I set out the small sand tray from my bag and spent ten minutes making prints with various things on the table and burying small items inside some plastic cups we have for making sand castles. Peter enjoyed this and was very playful, laughing when I found what he had buried and trying to guess what I was putting in my pot. He wanted to go to the park and Julia told him we could, when she had finished the ironing. He managed this deferment well and Julia gave him a drink and some fruit while he was waiting.

Once at the park, he and Julia repeated some role play developed during another visit. Peter was the pancake shop owner. He positioned himself behind a small counter beneath the slide and pretended to gather ingredients and mix the batter. He asked her what flavour she wanted and went to the back of the 'shop' to check if he had the right one. He cooked and served the pancakes and a cup of coffee and asked her for £3. During this, he was playful, confident and competent and in charge of the food. He was making and giving it to us and in doing so, was gaining a different meaning about having food – that he could give it out, rather than always being the one waiting to be given it. He moved from here to the small bike that was on a spring coil so that it bounced when it was sat on. With Julia's encouragement, he bounced hard, going 'fast' on the bike and they laughed together. Then Julia needed to take a phone call. The family's car was in the garage being serviced. She told Peter she needed to talk to the garage. Peter bounced on the bike a few more times and told me it was broken and we needed to get the 'garage man'. He went over to the corner of the play area to find him but returned telling me that the garage man couldn't come and I would have to fix it. He told me I could use the man's tool box and that I should get started quickly! I checked the headlights on the bike and said I needed to replace the bulbs. I asked Peter to see if they were working but they weren't. I pretended to check the switches, but they still didn't work. Peter told me I needed to go to the 'shop' to get a new steering wheel. I tried to fit it and told him I needed a number one screwdriver and asked him to fetch one from the same shop. We continued like this for around ten minutes and it was a wonderful piece of co-constructed play which showed Peter's developing resilience and sense of agency.

I saw his play as a metaphor for the shift from him needing to be helped, through us working together, towards him finding resolutions for himself. Part of this resolution was his recognition that Julia was an adult he could trust to take care of him and keep him safe. His attachment to her was much stronger than his relationship with David, which was taking longer to establish. Peter's experience showed him that men can be frightening, loud and aggressive, if not physically, then in their general demeanour. David was very different, but the shift in the family dynamics from two to three had unsettled him and Peter had picked this up and was unsure of David. Sometimes, things went well between them but at other times there was tension. Peter had talked of monsters coming to get him and his constant need for food had returned; it seemed that one had become the other so that the hunger within was the monster he believed he was. The monster was also external to him, symbolic of all those adults who had frightened him and led him to believe he was the 'naughty' boy who had caused their unreasonable reaction. In part, this had been laid to rest through Julia's containment and nurture of him but with the tension between him and David, it was present again. During our next session, we stayed in the house and his play was focused on seeing the monster at the window, hiding from it and running away. He shut the curtains and the door to keep the monster at bay, and shouted 'Go away monster, you can't get me. I'm safe in my house;' a symbolic house, created with Julia who could accept him as he was and so contain his inner monster. Both Peter and David were struggling with being the third person in the dynamic but it was David who was feeling left out as the attachment between Peter and Julia grew stronger.

I spent some time with David, and it became clear that he was feeling very isolated and he was able to reflect on the significance of these feelings in relation to his earlier life experiences. He was due to spend a day a week at home with Peter so we agreed to go out for a walk in the nearby woods the following week. The path to the woods started with open grass areas studded with trees and shrubs and passed through denser pine trees, eventually coming out onto the top of a hill which overlooked the valley below. David presented as quite a serious and self-contained man and our conversation had uncovered a childhood self who had not really had the opportunity to be a playful small boy and I wanted to see if, together, we could uncover this. As we walked down the path, I 'wondered' aloud if there might be monsters in the woods. Peter said I should close my eyes and they would hide. He was creating his own alliance with David, and David responded by taking him by the hand and running into the trees to hide, laughing at the noise they were making trampling over twigs on the ground. When I had counted loudly to 20 I went in search of them, keeping up a loud commentary about how I couldn't see them and wondering if I would ever find them. This brought Peter out from the trees, giggling and calling to me, afraid I really wouldn't be able to find him and making sure I did! After that we took it in turns to be the monster, sometimes hiding, sometimes fighting each other, but with Peter and David staying together, recreating the domestic triad in a safe way, firmly establishing their alliance and feeling able to experiment with it safely because I could be cast in the role of the third person, the 'mummy', without disastrous consequences. It showed them that there was a way three could be together without one being excluded. Although there were other people around us, we had together created our own therapeutic alliance with symbolic walls around our play. To those passing, we were just a family playing in the woods. The personal meanings of our play were not evident to them and they did not encroach on the play, we merely exchanged friendly greetings and passed on by. In fact, I think the presence of others served to anchor the play in reality, to serve as a bridge between our 'inner' play and the outer, ever present and real world around us.

When we reached the hilltop, we sat for a while on a bench at the edge, overlooking the valley below to regain our breath and some energy! Peter wanted to go to the edge to look down more directly below the hill so David went with him. Far below there were animals in the field and they began to sneak down the hillside to see if they could creep up on them. They disappeared below the hill line, only to reappear seconds later, shrieking and running back up the hill, chased by invisible wolves! Just as they neared the top, David scooped Peter into his arms and ran to the bench sitting down and holding Peter tightly against him, saying, 'Phew, I saved you from the wolves!' Peter squealed with delight and they repeated this play several more times until David was exhausted and had to rest. It had been a privilege to witness this, to see that together they had created the possibility for a different more mutually fulfilling relationship based on trust in each other. Peter had experienced David's strength being used to protect and not harm him and had had an embodied experience of maleness that was positive and allowed him to feel the possibility of his own strength as a protective factor. In our play together, Peter had experienced joy and pleasure and delighted in his own physicality. Although it would not be plain sailing for him and David, there had been some transformation within their relationship and over the next few months, their attachment to each other strengthened enough to survive the occasions when David's own monsters intruded and upset the fragile equilibrium of their new found alliance.

I do not believe we could have had such powerful experiences indoors. Peter was already developing a place attachment with the nearby park and was becoming familiar with the route to it and all that was there. Jungle Joe's presented opportunities for significant physical challenge which took Peter to the place between elation and fear, where real transformation can begin. The woods provided us with a neutral space; it belonged to none of us and so was a safe place for experimentation, for testing a newly formed alliance within the safety of a known and trusted one, that between Peter and myself. It provided us with a rich playground full of possibility where we not only physically played out fears and anxieties, but also the complex dynamics that exist between three people in a relationship. Peter had been able to trust not only his body self, but also his father's, to experience him as containing, both physically and emotionally, and to see and feel another way for a man to be, a potential future self.

CASE STUDY 3: MICHAEL

Michael was referred to me by his school, a specialist residential placement for boys with complex social, emotional and behavioural (SEB) needs. He was 11 at the start of the play therapy. Michael had experienced the loss of a number of members of his family following the separation of his birth parents and was living with his mother when I met him, having little or no contact with his siblings and birth father. It was believed that in his early years he had suffered from neglect and emotional abuse and there was also a concern that he may have witnessed sexual violence towards his mother. His learning was delayed due to some specific language and learning difficulties and he found friendships hard to make and sustain unless they were with significantly younger children. The staff at his school were concerned because they felt he existed in a world of his own, appeared to have very low self-esteem and isolated himself from others.

Settling

From his early sessions with me it was clear that Michael had no real sense of himself in any domain. He seemed unable to say anything about himself, positive or negative, and the main theme of his play was looking after others, making them food, caring for them when they were ill and celebrating their birthdays. His mother's own very difficult history manifested itself somatically and she seemed always to be unwell. Her needs were always put before Michael's and she discussed her medical issues in detail, leaving him anxious about her future. In tending to the needs of the puppets he was taking on a familiar role, just as small children do in their early play activities. Making food for us both to share reflected his need for the nurture and attunement that he had been denied and it created a bond between us.

Developing this early bond into a therapeutic alliance with Michael was difficult because although he was eager to come to the sessions, was always polite and engaged with the resources in a way which held significance and meaning for him, he was emotionally 'flat'. It wasn't that his mood was low, but in the session, he would explore some quite challenging issues without ever seeming to experience the emotional significance of them. His language needs meant that he did not necessarily have the words to describe how he might be feeling but it was not just this. When I wondered aloud about how he felt, he always said he didn't know, which he genuinely didn't since his feelings had never been taken in to account or validated. Trying to gauge his level of trust in me was difficult because I wasn't sure that we had a relationship in its usual sense, but we reached a point where I think he felt very comfortable with me.

In preparing food for the characters he had created, Michael also returned to early messy play, using paint, glitter and glue to mix soups, stews, various smoothies and special potions to heal or to cheer his characters up, just as he was needed to bear witness to his mother's illnesses and to be the one to keep her in good cheer. He told me he was using 'chemistry' to get the mixture right, measuring out drops of colour, always careful, taking the mixture just to the top of the bowl or bottle, decanting it into other pots and all the time experimenting with containment, trying to find an identity. Often he would elicit my help to stir, to fetch new 'ingredients' or to add 'special' ones. I commented on the glitter in the potion, suggested it was like people, full of different bits that made them interesting and unique. He rarely responded to any reflections but kept up a running commentary on his activities, telling me which character the mixture was for and how it would help them.

Around this time, Michael and his mother moved into her new partner's house. In his subsequent puppet play, there was a marriage of his two main characters. One of the other smaller puppets was upset, and Michael covered its ears and whispered to me, 'He's sad because his home caught fire and his mum and dad'…at this point he raised his eyes upward and I asked 'Heaven?' and he nodded. 'Oh!' I said, 'the house caught fire and the mum and dad died. That was very sad'. He gave the big puppet couple some babies so they could snuggle up, and wrapped a blanket around them, containing them and keeping the new family together.

I felt that somehow, through this, we had finally established our alliance and the fact that I needed this concrete evidence of his trust in me was something that perplexed me, but it was something which I believe he needed from his mother. He needed a tangible demonstration of her regard for him, not as someone to care for her but as someone she cared for, and could contain and keep safe.

Transition

Over the next few months, Michael continued to make his mixtures and potions although he now created these in a big bowl and a plastic tray and moved from a table at the side of the room to the main table in the middle as if he was now prepared to take centre stage. He left the puppets on a chair and began to create complex games with the vehicles and animals, which may well have been inspired by the computer games the boys played sometimes during their 'down' time in the evenings. The emergent themes were connected with rescuing, submerging things in a gooey mixture of paint and finding them again, building barriers and traps and avoiding dangerous animals. I felt he was working through the changing dynamics in his family. His mother was preoccupied with her partner and although Michael got on well with him and they spent time doing things together, as with Peter, in a family of three, someone always seemed to feel left out. His mother was protective of her time alone with her partner and I felt that for Michael, the relationship appeared as a barrier between him and his mother and he was also struggling to find a place in the new family relationship.

As time progressed, our interactions became more playful and rather than Michael keeping up a commentary on activities, we entered into a dialogue reminiscent of the early play between the mother figure and an infant. He would give me my role in the game but would offer me the opportunity to choose things to be or to have. I usually requested his help in choosing, and asked his advice about what might be best. I commented on all the aspects of our play that he knew a lot about and gradually he began to see himself as someone who had a purpose and abilities beyond helping and taking care of things. He was beginning to construct a new identity and this was reflected in my gaining a stronger sense of who Michael was. The school staff commented that he was less isolated and had begun to play with another boy. His relationship with his key worker and teacher had always been positive but he was also now able to make stronger connections with other staff members.

The school was surrounded by a sports field, a play area and a small copse that led down to an old quarry which the boys mainly used in the evenings and at weekends when they were boarding. The sports field had two covered sandpits, one close to the room where we had our sessions and one right across the other side, and the play area had a wooden sailing ship, a small hill with a slide over the top and a pipe tunnel through it. During lesson times, unless one of the boys was distressed or upset, there was generally no one in these areas as the hard play areas where PE took place were around the other side of the school. Michael and I had talked about using these outdoor areas and as his sense of self grew stronger, he showed more interest in leaving the playroom. I had a tray which contained my outdoor kit – a large thick plastic groundsheet, six metal tent awning poles, a selection of guy lines, plastic tent pegs and a mallet, a small plastic scoop, waterproofs, and a digital camera for recording images so that we left the land as we had found it. In addition to this, Michael knew he could take any of the indoor resources outside.

The session before he decided to go outside was quite extraordinary. The main table had always been half covered with a white plastic cloth and was the 'art' area. Michael gathered all the small bottles of paint together and began to pour and mix the colours in a bowl. He filled it to the absolute brim as always but then slowly continued to add more paint until it started to overflow. He continued carefully adding more paint until there was a lake of it on the table. He put four vehicles around the bottom of the bowl as a barrier; two sports cars, a police 4 x 4 and an RAC rescue truck, the latter two of which were present in every game we played. The paint oozed through this barrier and he added large sequins, and a wall of lentils around the edge. He continued to add water to the bowl so that the paint soon covered the smaller cars and began to creep beyond the lentil barrier. He said he needed to keep the paint from flowing off the table and asked me to help him put the paint pots around the edge; another border or barricade. He found some porridge oats in a small container and mixed them with water to form a sticky goo. When the paint bled through the bottles, he used this to form yet another barrier. I was caught by the dynamic nature of this creation and by our shared excitement of watching the paint escape through each barrier that was constructed.

There was such a potential of symbolism within it. His very essence, the new self he had created was growing and pushing through the barriers and breaking out. There were two vehicles that had been ever present in his play, symbolic of the rescuer and the protector, perhaps the roles played by his mother and partner within the triad of their family relationships or those played by myself and his keyworker, either way, they were roles which he had less need of now. Maybe they even represented the two of us, together containing the feelings which overwhelmed him. This session was transformative – something had shifted both in Michael himself and in the nature of our relationship. It had moved to a new, more equal, footing and I felt Michael knew he could trust me with his new and still fragile sense of who he might be.

The following session Michael wanted to go outside, close to the playroom among some trees. He wanted to tie the guy lines to the tree trunks and stretch them through the branches to demarcate his play area. He asked me to hold one end of each line as he tied the other. Relating this to his previous session with paint and the barrier of lentils, bottles and porridge, I began to think about schemas and the work of Cath Arnold and the Penn Green team on schemas and emotions (2010). Much of what Michael had been doing with his potions and mixtures was a physical representation of emotional containment, and the holding of the guy lines suggested his wish to stay connected, to step into an outer world but with the safety of the connection to me, symbolic of his inner world. The following session he wanted to go outside again, but this time further from the playroom. Once again, he used the guy lines but this time, although he asked me to hold them, he wanted me to peg them into the ground, to connect him more firmly to this outer world. He spent some time tying two figures onto the lines, Spiderman and a soldier, which I had come to think was symbolic of himself, thereby anchoring them firmly in the outside world. After this, he moved off to the play area, climbing the slide and beckoning for me to climb the steps, join him and walk down the slide as if we were crossing a bridge. From here he went to the trampoline and proudly showed me how he could bounce and drop into a sitting position and then bounce and land face down. He showed me he could enjoy what his body could do, developing an understanding of its capacity and strength.

Transformation

Shortly after this Michael's mother and her partner started arguing and talked about taking time away from each other. Michael took the RAC rescue truck, a large crane and a large cement mixture out quite some distance from the playroom to where there was a pile of wood chippings. He made a small fence on one side above the base of the pile as if it were a ledge. He tied a guy line to the RAC truck and sitting on the top of the pile, lowered it down until it was hanging through the fence over the edge of the ledge. He said it just balanced there, but could crash down at any moment. He tied off the line to a large stick and pushed this into the chippings to secure the truck. Then he tied the cement mixer and the crane to either end of another line and put them on the top of the pile. He pushed the crane off one side while he held onto the cement mixer at the top. The crane rolled down and began to pull the cement mixture over the top. Michael held the cement mixer fast, then began to push it down the other side so that the crane began to rise back to the top. He held the cement mixer for a minute or so, pushing in down deep into the chippings to stop it from being pulled back over the top by the weight of the crane. Then he let it go and the crane pulled it over the top and down the other side. He sat upright gazing into the distance and I sat with him, feeling the pain of the impending separation. We sat in silence for some minutes and I reflected to him that something inside him was hurting and he was sad. He looked at me briefly, got up and walked back to the playroom. I believe this was the first time he had been in touch with his feelings and it was a profound moment for both of us. Back in the playroom, he made a circle of play dough and marked out a smiley face on it then took a pencil and pushed it through the face, destroying the smile, as his own happiness had been destroyed.

Michael and I spent many sessions outside as he and his mother moved into a new house and they resumed their relationship together. He had just become used to having her attention when she met another new partner. But Michael was much more resilient now with a stronger sense of who he was and able to cope better with this new relationship. There were also other things he was grappling with related to his life at school and he processed some very deeply personal issues. In our penultimate session, we went to the area farthest from the school and he used the poles and guy lines to fence off and area off the woodland which he called the 'safe place'. He laid out the groundsheet and put down four of the puppets he had brought which he used to tell a story, a metaphor for something in his earlier life experience. He finished the story and got up and wandered off to check the fences. From some distance away but from where we could still see each other, he told me about something he had seen several years before and of which he had not been able to make any sense, a very eleventh-hour event! However, he had been able to bring his past experience to the present to process it so that together we might find some resolution to it. I was reminded of a social worker friend of mine who had told me once that there were many clients who spent the whole visit talking about nothing in particular, only to disclose some grizzly scenario that had occurred just as she was leaving the house!

Michael used the outdoors as a concrete way of stepping into the light and bridging his inner and outer worlds. I believe he was able to undergo the transformations he did because outside was his familiar territory, his world, a world to which he had a strong attachment and felt at home in. The playroom had provided him with a physical containment for the long time it took us to develop the containing therapeutic alliance. Once this was established, he could begin to take a risk and discover who he was. From here he could venture forth and begin to make some connections between his past and present experiences and begin to find some resolutions.

Appendix

Outdoor Kit

If a child chooses to work outside, they may take any of the indoor resources with them and I have additional items as follows:

- a large thick plastic groundsheet
- variously sized waterproof trousers, jackets and jumpers (hats and sunscreen for summer)
- a trowel, scoop and small spade
- a set of tent awning extensions poles
- various guy ropes and lengths of thick string
- some plastic tent pegs and a small mallet
- two plastic trays for carrying resources
- an old towel
- a small first aid kit, mobile phone and penknife (therapist only).

As we 'leave nature as we found it', I also carry a small digital camera for photographing creations should the child wish them to be recorded. To date, none of my resources have been spoiled by being used outside. Small-world toys and vehicles are easily washable, the beanbag I have is designed for outdoor use and the puppets can be carefully hand washed.

References

About Forest School Camps (2013) Available at www.fsc.org.uk/about.htm, accessed on 3 November 2013.

Alderson, P. (2008) *Young Children's Rights – Exploring Beliefs, Principles and Practice.* London: Jessica Kingsley Publishers.

Arnold, C. and the Penn Green Team (2010) *Understanding Schemas and Emotions in Early Childhood.* London: Sage Publications.

Athey, C. *Extending Thought in Young Children: A Parent–Teacher Partnership.* London: Sage.

Australian Child Wellbeing (2013) *Australian Child Wellbeing Project.* Available at http://australianchildwellbeing.com.au, accessed on 5 September 2013.

Axline, V. (1964) *Dibs: In Search of Self.* USA: Pelican Books.

Axline, V. (1969) *Play Therapy.* Canada: Ballantyne Books.

BACP (2013) *Framework for Good Practice in Counselling and Psychotherapy.* Available at www.bacp.co.uk/admin/structure/files/pdf/9479_ethical%20framework%20jan2013.pdf, accessed on 12 September 2013.

Bailey, A. and Barnes, S. (2009) 'Where Do I Fit In? Children's Spaces and Places.' In R. Eke, H. Butcher and M. Lee (eds) *Whose Childhood Is It? The Roles of Children, Adults and Policy Makers.* London: Continuum.

Bailey, R. (2011) *Letting Children Be Children: Report of an Independent Review of the Commercialisation and Sexualisation of Childhood.* Available at www.gov.uk/government/uploads/system/uploads/attachment_data/file/175418/Bailey_Review.pdf, accessed on 17 July 2013.

BAPT (2008) *An Ethical Basis for Good Practice in Play Therapy* (3rd edition). Weybridge: BAPT.

Beder, S., Varney, W. and Gosden, R. (2009) *This Little Kiddy Went to Market; The Corporate Capture of Childhood.* London: Pluto Books.

Bell, G. (2004) *The Permaculture Garden.* Hampshire: Permanent Publications.

Berger, R. and Lahad, M. (2013) *The Healing Forest in Post-Crisis Work with Children.* London: Jessica Kingsley Publishers.

Bond, T. (2004) 'Ethical guidelines for researching counselling and psychotherapy.' *Counselling and Psychotherapy Research: linking research with practice 4,* 2 10–19.

Bowlby, J. (1988) *The Secure Base: Clinical Applications of Attachment Theory.* London: Routledge.

Briggs, A. (2011) *Reforming Acts.* Available at www.bbc.co.uk/history/british/victorians/reforming_acts_01.shtml#four, accessed on 12 June 2013.

Bruce, T. (2001) *Learning Through Play: Babies, Toddlers and the Foundation Years.* London: Hodder Arnold.

Bruce, T. (2011) 'Froebel Today.' In L. Miller and L. Pound (eds) *Theories and Approaches to Learning in the Early Years. Critical Issues in the Early Years.* London: Sage.

Buckingham, D. (2011) *Premature Sexualisation: Understanding the Risks.* NSPCC. Available at www.nspcc.org.uk/Inform/policyandpublicaffairs/consultations/2011/premature_sexualisation_pdf_wdf81574.pdf, accessed on 21 September 2013.

Burnham, J. (1998) Foreword in J. Wilson *Child-Focused Practice: A Collaborative Systemic Approach.* London: Karnac Books.

Butcher, H. and Andrews, J. (2009) 'How Well Am I Doing On MY Outcomes?' In R. Eke, H. Butcher and M. Lee (eds) *Whose Childhood Is It? The Roles of Children, Adults and Policy Makers.* London: Continuum.

Byron, T. 2008. *Safer Children in a Digital World: The report of the Byron Review 2008.* London: DCSF.

Byron, T. 2010. *Do we have safer children in a digital world? A review of progress since the Byron Review.* London: DCSF.

Cattanach, A. (1999) 'Co-construction.' In A. Cattanach (ed.) *Play Therapy Process in the Arts Therapies.* London: Jessica Kingsley Publishers.

Cattanach, A. (2003) *Introduction to Play Therapy.* Hove: Bruner-Routledge.

The Children's Society (2008) *The 2008 Survey.* Available at www.childrenssociety.org.uk/what-we-do/research/initiatives/well-being/background-programme/2008-survey, accessed on 12 July 2013.

Chown, M. (1963) *Essays on Play.* Unpublished.

Clayton, P. (2012) *Octavia Hill, Social Reformer and Co-founder of The National Trust.* Hampshire: Pitkin Publishing.

The Connected Baby (2011) Directed by Zeedyk, S. [DVD] Edinburgh: British Psychological Society.

Coy, M. (2011) *Understanding the Impact of Sexualised Images on Young People. Premature sexualisation: Understanding the Risks.* NSPCC. Available at www.nspcc.org.uk/Inform/policyandpublicaffairs/consultations/2011/premature_sexualisation_pdf_wdf81574.pdf, accessed on 21 September 2013.

Damasio, A. (2000) *The Feeling of What Happens: Body, Emotion and the Making of Consciousness.* London: Vintage.

Daniels, D. and Jenkins, P. (2010) *Therapy with Children: Children's Rights, Confidentiality and the Law* (2nd edition) *Ethics in Practice* (series ed. T. Bond). London: Sage.

DCSF/DCMS (2009) *The Impact of the Commercial World on Children's Wellbeing*. Nottingham: DCSF Publications.

Diener, E. (2000) 'Subjective well-being: the science of happiness, and a proposed national index.' *American Psychologist 55*, 1, 34–43.

Department of Work and Pensions (2013) *Households Below Average Income (HBAI)*. Available at www.gov.uk/government/collections/households-below-average-income-hbai--2, accessed on 14 October 2013.

Drauglis, E. (2009) *NUT Advice on Using Commercial Material in School*. UK: National Union of Teachers.

Duke of Edinburgh's Award (2013) Available at www.dofe.org, accessed on 2 November 2013.

Ecclestone, K. and Hayes, D. (2009) *The Dangerous Rise of Therapeutic Education*. London: Routledge.

Ecopsychology UK (2013) Available at www.ecopsychology.org.uk, accessed on 3 November 2013.

Egan, G. (2002) *The Skilled Helper – A Problem-Management and Opportunity-Development Approach to Helping* (7th edition). Pacific Grove, CA: Brookes/Cole.

Erikson, E. (1995) *Childhood and Society*. London: Vintage.

ET Seton Institute *History of the Woodcraft Movement*. Available at http://etsetoninstitute.org/history-of-the-woodcraft-movement, accessed 23 October 2013.

Fairlie S. (2009) 'A short history of enclosure in Britain.' *The Land 7*, Summer 2009, 16–31.

Federal Interagency Forum on Child and Family Statistics (2011) *America's Children: Key National Indicators of Well-Being, 2011*. Washington, DC: US Government Printing Office.

Find a Montessori school (2013). Available at www.montessori.org.uk/msa/find_a_school, accessed on 10 November 2013.

Fionda, J. (2009) 'Children, Young People and the Law.' In H. Montgomery and M. Kellet (eds) *Children and Young People's Worlds: Developing Frameworks for Integrated Practice*. Bristol: Policy Press.

First Peoples Worldwide. *About us*. Available at www.firstpeoples.org/about-us/about-us, accessed on 27 October 2013.

France, A. (2010) 'The Commercialization of Childhood.' *The View* Spring/Summer 12–13. Available at www.lboro.ac.uk/research/view/ss10/pdf/theview-springsummer2010.pdf, accessed on 12 August 2013.

Freeman, M. (2009) 'Fellowship, service and the "spirit of adventure": the Religious Society of Friends and the outdoor movement in Britain c1900–1950.' *Quaker Studies 14*, 71–92. Available at http://eprints.gla.ac.uk/29901/1/29901.pdf, accessed on 23 July 2013.

Frost, J. L. (2010) *A History of Children's Play and Play Environments – Towards a Contemporary Child-Saving Movement.* New York: Routledge.

Garner, B. P. and Bergan, D. (2006) 'Play Development from Birth to Age Four.' In D. P. Fromberg and D. Bergen (eds) *Play from Birth to Twelve: Contexts, Perspectives and Meanings* (2nd edition). London: Routledge.

Geddes, H. (2006) *Attachment in the Classroom.* London: Worth Publishing.

Gerhardt, S. (2004) *Why Love Matters: How Affection Shapes a Baby's Brain.* London: Routledge.

Gill, R. (2011) *Understanding the Impact of Sexualised Images on Young People, Premature Sexualisation: Understanding the Risks.* NSPCC. Available at www.nspcc.org.uk/Inform/policyandpublicaffairs/consultations/2011/premature_sexualisation_pdf_wdf81574.pdf, accessed on 21 September 2013.

Gill, T. (2007) *No Fear: Growing Up in a Risk Averse Society.* London: Calouste Gulbenkian Foundation.

Girlguiding (2013) Available at www.girlguiding.org.uk/about-us/what-makes-guiding-special.aspx, accessed on 23 September 2013.

Goddard Blythe, S. (2008) *What Babies and Children Really Need.* Stroud: Hawthorn Press.

Goldberg, S. (2000) *Attachment and Development.* London: Arnold.

Goodman, A. and Gregg, P. (2010) *Poorer children's educational attainment: how important are attitudes and behaviour?* Available at www.jrf.org.uk/sites/files/jrf/poorer-children-education-full.pdf, accessed on 3 June 2013.

Gordonstoun School History (2013). Available at: www.gordonstoun.org.uk/school-history, accessed on 3 November 2013.

The Guardian (Friday 16 August 2013) *'Scottish teenager "killed himself over online blackmail threats"'* Available at www.theguardian.com/uk-news/2013/aug/16/scottish-teenager-online-blackmail-skype, accessed on 16 August 2013.

Grainger, R. (1999) *Researching the Arts Therapies – A Dramatherapist's Perspective.* London: Jessica Kingsley Publishers.

Gray, C. and Macblain, S. (2012) *Learning Theories in Childhood.* London: Sage.

Grayson, J. H. *Grith Fyrd Camps – An Experiment in Community Building.* Available at www.fsc.org.uk/archive/Grith_Fyrd_Camps_1934.pdf, accessed on 28 October 2013.

Hackett, J. (2008) Speech to the Institute for Occupational Safety and Health on 8 May 2008. Available at www.hse.gov.uk/aboutus/speeches/transcripts/iosh/80508.htm, accessed on 17 July 2013.

Harper, P. *The Early Years of Woodcraft Folk 1925–1985*. Available at http://vimeo.com/channels/woodcraftfolk/38327735, accessed on 8 October 2013.

Health and Social Care Information Centre (2012) *Health Survey for England 2011*. Available at www.hscic.gov.uk/catalogue/PUB09300, accessed on 12 October 2013.

Health and Social Care Information Centre (2013) *Statistics on Obesity, Physical Activity and Diet: England 2013*. Available at https://catalogue.ic.nhs.uk/publications/public-health/obesity/obes-phys-acti-diet-eng-2013/obes-phys-acti-diet-eng-2013-rep.pdf, accessed on 23 September 2013.

Hewitt, D. (2009*) Intensive Interaction Priorities and Principles* [PowerPoint]. Available at www.nicurriculum.org.uk/docs/inclusion_and_sen/training_events/intensive_interaction_pmld, accessed on 28 October 2013.

Hill, O. (1875) *Homes of the London Poor*. Digitally reprinted in 2010 by Cambridge University Press, New York. Available at http://assets.cambridge.org/97811080/24556/copyright/9781108024556_copyright_info.pdf, accessed on 10 June 2013.

HM Treasury (2003) *Every Child Matters*. CM5860. London: TSO. Available at www.education.gov.uk/publications/eOrderingDownload/DFES108 12004.pdf, accessed on 3 July 2013.

Howe, D., Brandon, M., Hinings, D. and Schofield, G. (1999) *Attachment Theory, Child Maltreatment and Family Support*. New York: Palgrave.

Huebner E. (1994) 'Preliminary development and validation of a multidimensional life satisfaction scale for children.' *Psychological Assessment 6*, 2, 149–158.

Hughes, D. (2006) *Building the Bonds of Attachment: Awakening Love in Deeply Troubled Children* (2nd edition). Oxford: Aronson.

Hunt, T. (2012) *Octavia Hill – Her Life and Legacy*. Available at www.nationaltrust.org.uk/article-1356393664070/, accessed on 7 July 2013.

Institute of Child Health (2013) *Half of all 7-year-olds not getting enough exercise*. Available at www.ucl.ac.uk/ich/ich-news/aug-13/article69, accessed on 2 September 2013.

Institute of Education (IOE), London (2009) *Institute of Education Archives Subject Guide No 3: Progressive Education*. Available at www.ioe.ac.uk/services/documents/SG3_Progressive_Education_(March_2009).pdf, accessed on 2 November 2013.

Isaacs, B. (2007) *Bringing the Montessori Approach to your Early Years Practice* (series ed. S. Green). London: Routledge.

Jack, G. (2010) 'Place matters: the significance of place attachments for children's well-being.' *British Journal of Social Work 40*, 755–771. Available at http://bjsw.oxfordjournals.org, accessed on 26 October 2013.

Jennings, S. (1999) *Introduction to Developmental Play Therapy*. London: Jessica Kingsley Publishers.

Jennings, S. (2005) *Creative Storytelling with Adults at Risk*. Milton Keynes: Speechmark.

Jennings, S. (2011) *Healthy Attachments and Neuro-Dramatic-Play*. London: Jessica Kingsley Publishers.

Jones, O. (2011) *Chavs: The Demonization of the Working Class*. London: Verso.

Jones, P (2011) 'What are Children's Rights? Contemporary Developments and Debates.' In P. Jones and G. Walker (eds) *Children's Rights in Practice*. London: Sage.

Jordan, M. and Marshall, H. (2010) 'Taking counselling and psychotherapy outside: destruction or enrichment of the therapeutic frame?' *European Journal of Psychotherapy & Counselling 12*, 4, 345–359.

Judge Smith, C. *John Hargrave – 'White Fox'*. Available at www.kibbokift.org/jhbio.html, accessed on 10 October 2013.

Kellet, M. (2011) *Children's Perspectives on Integrated Services*. Basingstoke: Palgrave MacMillan.

Knight, S. (2009) *Forest Schools and Outdoor Learning in the Early Years*. London: Sage.

Knight, S. (2011) *Forest School for All*. London: Sage.

Landreth, G. (2002) *Play Therapy: The Art of the Relationship* (2nd edition). Hove: Brunner-Routledge.

Latent Existence (17 March 2012) *Bedroom tax: just stop smoking and drinking says housing association*. Available at www.latentexistence.me.uk/bedroom-tax-just-stop-smoking-and-drinking-says-housing-association, accessed on 26 October 2013.

Layard, R. and Dunn, J. (2009) *A Good Childhood: Searching for Values in a Competitive Age*. London: Penguin.

Lee M. and Eke R. (2009) 'Children and screens'. In Eke R., Butcher H. and Lee M. (eds) *Whose Childhood Is It? The roles of children, adults and policy makers*. London: Continuum International Publishing Group.

Lemma, A. (2010) 'The power of relationship: a study of key working as an intervention with traumatised young people.' *Journal of Social Work Practice 24*, 4, 409–427. Available at http://dx.doi.org/10.1080/0265 0533.2010.496965, accessed on 9 September 2011.

Lewis Herman, J. (2001) *Trauma and Recovery: From Domestic Abuse to Political Terror*. London: Pandora.

Liepman, L. (1994) *Your Child's Sensory World*. Baltimore, MD: Penguin.

Livingstone, S., Kirmil, L., Ponte, C., Staksrud, E. and EU Kids Online Network (2013) *In their Own Words: What Bothers Children Online.* Available at www.lse.ac.uk/media@lse/research/EUKidsOnline/EU%20Kids%20III/Reports/Intheirownwords020213.pdf, accessed on 25 August 2013.

Louv, R. (2005) *Last Child in the Woods – Saving Our Children from Nature-Deficit Disorder.* London: Atlantic Books.

Low, S. and Barnes, A. (20 June 2012) *'Jamie Oliver "lost faith" with ministers over schools meals campaign.'* The Independent. Available at www.independent.co.uk/news/uk/politics/jamie-oliver-lost-faith-with-ministers-over-school-meals-campaign-7869798.html, accessed on 23 July 2013.

McCarthy, D. (2012) *A Manual of Dynamic Play Therapy: Helping Things Fall Apart, The Paradox of Play.* London: Jessica Kingsley Publishers.

McFarlane, P. (2012) *Creative Drama for Emotional Support.* London: Jessica Kingsley Publishers.

McLean, P.D. (1990) *The Triune Brain in Evolution: Role in Paleocerebral Functions.* Norwell, MA: Kluwer Academic Publishers.

McMahon, L. (1992) *The Handbook of Play Therapy.* London: Routledge.

Meins, E., Fernyhough, C., Wainwright, R., Clark-Carter, D., Das Gupta, M., Fradley, E. and Tuckey, M. (2003) 'Pathways to understanding mind: construct, validity and predictive validity of maternal mind mindedness.' *Child Development 74*, 4, 1194–1211.

Miller, A. (1987) *The Drama of Being a Child.* London: Virago.

MIND (2007) *Ecotherapy – the green agenda for mental health.* Available at www.mind.org.uk/media/273470/ecotherapy.pdf, accessed on 27 September 2013.

Molnar, A. (2005) *School Commercialism: From Democratic Ideal to Market Commodity.* New York: Routledge.

Music G. (2011) *Nurturing Natures – Attachment and Children's Emotional, Sociocultural and Brain Development.* Hove: Psychology Press.

National Trust (2013) *50 things to do before you're 11¾.* Available at www.50things.org.uk, accessed on 25 August 2013.

Naess, A. (2005) *Ecology of Wisdom: Writings by Arne Naess.* Edited by A. Grengson and B. Devall. Berkeley, CA: Counterpoint.

Nature Nurture (2011). Available at http://naturenurture.org.uk/index.html, accessed on 23 September 2013.

The Nature Therapy Center (2010). Available at www.naturetherapy.org.il/index.php?lang=en, accessed on 23 July 2013.

NHS Information Centre (2011) *Health Survey for England: 2011.* Available at https://catalogue.ic.nhs.uk/publications/public-health/surveys/heal-surv-eng-2011/HSE2011-Sum-bklet.pdf, accessed on 29 June 2013.

Norman, S. (2009) 'Give Sure Start a Fair Start.' In R. Eke, H. Butcher and M. Lee (eds) *Whose Childhood Is It? The Roles of Children, Adults and Policy Makers.* London: Continuum.

NSPCC (2011) *Help and Advice.* Available at www.nspcc.org.uk/help-and-advice/help_and_advice_hub_wdh71748.html, accessed on 25 August 2013.

Oaklander, V. (1988) *Windows to Our Children.* New York: The Gestalt Journal Press.

OFCOM (2004) *Television Advertising of Food and Drink Products to Children.* Available at http://stakeholders.ofcom.org.uk/consultations/foodads_new/statement, accessed on 12 July 2013.

O'Hara, M. (2013) *Deprivation, Depression and Demonization Part of Daily Struggle.* Available at www.jrf.org.uk/austerity-birmingham, accessed on 24 September 2013.

Orbach, S. (2004) 'The Body in Clinical Practice.' In K. White (ed.) *Touch, Attachment and the Body.* London: Karnac Books.

Outward Bound. *Outward Bound's Founders.* Available at www.outwardbound.net/about-us/history/outward-bounds-founders, accessed on 7 November 2013.

Pearce, C. (2009) *A Short Introduction to Attachment and Attachment Disorder.* London: Jessica Kingsley Publishers.

Perry, B. (2002) *The Amazing Human Brain and Human Development.* Available at www.childtraumaacademy.com/amazing_brain/lesson01/page01.html, accessed on 13 October 2013.

Play England (2013) *Unwelcoming Communities Stop Children Playing Out.* Available at www.playengland.org.uk/news/2013/08/unwelcoming-communities-stop-children-playing-out.aspx, accessed on 5 September 2013.

Porter, L. (2006) *Behaviour in Schools* (2nd edition). Berkshire: Open University Press.

Prince, R. (29 March 2009) *'David Cameron: family values the key to responsible society' The Telegraph.* Available at www.telegraph.co.uk/news/politics/5070968/David-Cameron-family-values-the-key-to-responsible-society.html, accessed on 28 July 2013.

Ramblers (2013) *Our History.* Available at www.ramblers.org.uk/about-us/our-history.aspx, accessed on 29 October 2013.

Records of the Forest School Camps. Available at http://archive.ioe.ac.uk/DServe/dserve.exe?dsqIni=Dserve.ini&dsqApp=Archive&dsqCmd=Show.tcl&dsqDb=Catalog&dsqPos=0&dsqSearch=(RefNo='fsc]'), accessed on 2 November 2013.

Rees, G., Pople, L. and Goswani, H. (2011) *Understanding Children's Well-Being.* Available at www.childrenssociety.org.uk/sites/default/files/tcs/research_docs/Economic%20Factors%20March%202011.pdf, accessed on 23 August 2013.

Rees, G., Goswami, H. and Pople, L. (2012) *The Good Childhood Report 2012.* Available at www.childrenssociety.org.uk/sites/default/files/tcs/good_childhood_report_2012_final_0.pdf, accessed 3 September 2013.

Rey, H. (1994) *Universals of Psychoanalysis in the Treatment of Psychotic and Borderline States.* London: Free Association Books.

Rogers, C. (1983) *Freedom to Learn for the 1980's.* Columbus, OH: Merrill.

Rogers, C. (2003) *Client-Centred Therapy: Its Current Practice, Implications and Theory.* London: Constable.

Rothschild, B. (2000) *The Body Remembers – The Psychophysiology of Trauma and Trauma Treatment.* New York: Norton.

Rothman, B. (2012) *The Battle for Kinder Scout Including the 1932 Mass Trespass.* Cheshire: Willow Publishing.

Round Square (2012) *Who We Are.* Available at www.roundsquare.org/who.php, accessed on 8 November 2013.

Ryan, V. and Wilson, K. (2000) *Case Studies in Non-directive Play Therapy.* London: Jessica Kingsley Publishers.

Santostefano, S. (2004) *Child Therapy in the Great Outdoors: A Relational View.* Jersey: The Analytic Press.

Saunders, L. (2 January 2013) *'Model in the making! Heidi Klum's daughter Leni looks every inch her mother's mini-me with matching scarf and bag.'* The Daily Mail. Available at www.dailymail.co.uk/tvshowbiz/article-2256353/Heidi-Klum-mini-daughter-Leni-strut-stuff-head-sushi-matching-outfits.html, accessed on 23 July 2013.

Seton, E.T. *Woodcraft is Lifecraft.* Available at http://etsetoninstitute.org/the-woodcraft-way, accessed on 24 October 2013.

Sherborne, V. (2001) *Developmental Movement for Children: Mainstream, Special Needs and Pre school.* London: Worth Publishing.

Smith, R. (2012) 'Milestones on the Path to Freedom.' In B. Rothman *The Bettle for Kinder Scout Including the 1932 Mass Tresspass.* Cheshire. Willow Publishing.

Steiner Waldorf. *What is Steiner Education?* Available at www.steinerwaldorf.org/whatissteinereducation.html, accessed on 4 November 2013.

Taylor, A., Kuo, E and Sullivan W. (2001) *Coping with ADD: The Surprising Connection to Green Play Settings.* Available at http://naturenurture.uk/pdf/greenspace%20positively%20impacts%20on%20the%20effects%20of%20ADHD.pdf, accessed on 12 September.

The Telegraph (29 August 2011) '*Couple threatened with fine over noisy four-year-old son.*' Available at www.telegraph.co.uk/news/newstopics/howaboutthat/8729161/Couple-threatened-with-fine-over-noisy-four-year-old-son.html, accessed on 12 July 2013.

Thrive Approach (2013) *The Thrive Approach.* Available at www.thriveapproach.co.uk, accessed on 23 September 2013.

Totton, N. (2003) *Body Psychotherapy – An Introduction.* Berkshire: Open University Press.

Tovey, H. (2007) *Playing Outdoors: Spaces and Places, Risks and Challenges.* Berkshire: Open University Press.

Trevarthen, C. (2004) 'Intimate Contact from Birth.' In K. White (ed.) *Touch, Attachment and the Body.* London: Karnac Books.

Trevithick, P. (2005) *Social Work Skills – A Practice Handbook* (2nd edition). Berkshire: Open University Press.

UNICEF (2007) 'Child poverty in perspective: an overview of child well-being in rich countries.' *Innocenti Report Card* 7, UNICEF Innocenti Research Centre, Florence.

UNICEF Office of Research (2013) 'Child well-being in rich countries: a comparative overview.' *Innocenti Report Card 11*, UNICEF Office of Research, Florence

Van der Kolk, B., McFarlane, A. C. and Weiseath, L. (eds) (1996) *Traumatic Stress: The Effects of Overwhelming Experiences on Mind, Body and Society.* London: Guildford Press.

Varney, W. and Beder, S. (2009) 'Turning Play into Business.' In S. Beder, W. Varney and R. Gosden (eds) *This Little Kiddy Went to Market: The Corporate Capture of Childhood.* London: Pluto Books.

Walter, N. (2010) *Living Dolls: The Return of Sexism.* London: Virago.

West, J. (1992) *Child Centred Play Therapy* (2nd edition). London: Arnold.

Wilderness Foundation United Kingdom (2012) Available at www.wildernessfoundation.org.uk/about-us, accessed on 23 October 2013.

Williams-Siegfredson, J. (2012) *Understanding the Danish Forest School Approach. Early Years Education in Practice.* London: Routledge.

Wilson, J. (2004) *Child-Focused Practice: A Collaborative Systemic Approach.* London: Karnac Books.

Wilson, K., Kendrick, P. and Ryan, V. (1992) *Play Therapy: A Non-directive Approach for Children and Adolescents.* London: Balliere and Tindall.

Winn, L. (2008) *Post Traumatic Stress Disorder and Dramatherapy – Treament and Risk Reduction.* London: Jessica Kingsley Publishers.

Winnicott, D. (1971) *Playing and Reality.* Hove: Brunner-Routledge.

Wood, H. (2013) *Young People and Pornography.* Available at www.vodafone.com/content/parents/expert-views/young_people_and_pornography.html, accessed on 15 September 2013.

Woodcraft Folk History (2010). Available at http://woodcraft.org.uk/history, accessed on 5 November 2013.

Young Minds (2013) *What is Post Traumatic Stress?* Available at www.youngminds.org.uk/for_children_young_people/whats_worrying_you/post_traumatic_stress/what_is_ptsd, accessed on 19 September 2013.

Young People Now (2005) *Young People and the Media.* Available at www.ipsos-mori.com/Assets/Docs/Archive/Polls/young-people-now.pdf, accessed on 20 September 2013.

Subject Index

Author Index